LEAD!

Be Inspired.
Inspire Others.

BEN RENSHAW

Balloonview

Testimonials

LEAD! fulfills its promise – to inspire. Ben Renshaw plays an important role in supporting the career journeys of many of the great leaders we have in the business today.

Richard Solomons, CEO InterContinental Hotels Group

At Heathrow, we have been transforming the passenger experience through world-class new facilities and collaborative ways of working. Ben Renshaw has been pivotal in coaching some of our most senior leaders and teams to deliver this change and achieve their potential. In LEAD! he shares many of the key points that resonate with our purpose and values as an organisation.

John-Holland Kaye, CEO Heathrow

Leaders need to inspire people to be at the top of their game… Ben has an ability to take people on a journey to make this possible.

Andy Cosslett, CEO Fitness First, Chairman of England Rugby 2015

The corporate world is filled with executives who have worked hard for years to reach the upper levels of management. They are intelligent, skilled, and even charismatic. But only a handful of them will ever reach the pinnacle. In LEAD! Ben Renshaw shows how in 50 concise steps you can accelerate your leadership development in meaningful ways. I encourage all executives to read this book.

Marshall Goldsmith, author of *What Got You Here Won't Get You There*, and corporate America's pre-eminent Executive Coach

The challenge for leaders is to focus on the crucial questions that will make the biggest difference. In LEAD! Ben Renshaw paints a rich landscape of what leaders need to ask in order to determine their and their organisation's destiny.

Graham Alexander, founder of The Alexander Partnership and author of *Tales From The Top* and *SuperCoaching*

Successful businesses are those that provide meaning at work for their employees. This requires companies to develop traits such as an invigorating purpose, connecting with DNA values and history and creating leaders who focus on self-actualisation. LEAD! is a great companion for leaders committed to being motivated and energised to create successful organisations.

Gurnek Bains, Chairman YSC, author of *Meaning Inc*

Leaders have a demanding set of responsibilities such as living by a clear set of values, liberating their people to take more accountability, acting collaboratively to produce greater job fulfillment … LEAD! encourages us to improve our leadership to meet these challenges and more.

Normand Boivin, COO Heathrow

In my book Corporate Voodoo, I explored the question, 'Why do many individuals keep resorting to learned behaviour, the habits and ideas that may have brought them success in the past, but which will leave them adrift in the fast–moving currents of the new economy?' This question is just as relevant today and it's great to see Ben Renshaw in LEAD! share a range of compelling ideas to inspire us to succeed.

René Carayol, author of *Corporate Voodoo* and *CEO Inspired Leaders Network*

We live in a digital age. However, we must not lose sight of the fact that the way to maximise the opportunities technology provides is through quality leadership. LEAD! is a powerful guide to help leaders rise to the challenges that lie ahead.

Pete Connor, Group IT Director, Home Retail Group

At its best leadership is about having a range of mountains to climb which stretches you to grow…it's then critical to get great talent around you in order to build momentum and deliver the business agenda. In LEAD! Ben focuses on these key elements and more to stretch you to be the best leader you can.

Nick Cullen, Group Supply Chain Director, Clarks

At Home Retail Group we are on an exciting transformation journey. Our success will largely be determined by the quality of our leaders and I know that LEAD! will inspire them along the way.

Julie Elder, Group HRD, Home Retail Group

Our simple truth at Planet Organic is that food should be authentic and ethical. This is true of leadership. In LEAD! Ben Renshaw captures so many truths about leadership that it will nourish your mind and body.

Renée Elliott, Founder Planet Organic

I believe that one of the most critical factors for success in organisations today is to have strong, inspirational leaders who can help people to do their best work and deliver transformation. LEAD! supports and challenges leaders to develop their leadership style and be better equipped for the future.

Sian Evans, Head of Talent & Development, Home Retail Group

The best leaders are instinctive, and lead from the heart and the head. It's great to see a book like LEAD! offer practical ways to do this and more. It's certainly what we look for in our energetic, creative and enthusiastic leaders at Sky.

Sophie Turner Laing, Sky Managing Director, Entertainment, News & Broadcast Operations

In our always-on, socially connected world, leaders need to get attention and pay attention more quickly than ever. The secret is to be able to inspire, and LEAD! is a brilliant guide to getting your message across in succinct, compelling and meaningful ways.

Mike Mathieson, CEO Cake

Here at Cookie Time brand, love and consumer satisfaction are non-negotiable. The way to bring these to life is through leadership. In LEAD! Ben Renshaw embraces the vital ingredients which will enable you to create your own brand love as a leader.

Michael Mayell, Founder Cookie Time

I believe that there are four critical factors in leadership – energy, empathy, intellect and values. LEAD! takes these qualities to the next level and reminds leaders about what is most important.

Will Morris, Group MD Retail, SSE

I work in a world of entrepreneurs who constantly need new sources of inspiration to fire their creativity and build better relationships. I welcome LEAD! as a companion along the journey.

Buggsi Patel, Chairman IHG Owners Association

At Heathrow we believe that the quality of our leadership will ensure we deliver our purpose of 'Making Every Journey Better'. Ben is a key strategic partner in developing our senior leaders and LEAD! is an inspiring illustration of his principles and practices.

Paula Stannett, HR Director Heathrow

Having been in a trusted partnership with Ben over 20 years he has been a constant source of inspiration for me and my leadership team…our values at myhotel are I.N.S.P.I.R.E and LEAD! will inspire us to create an even better future.

Andreas Thrasyvolou, Founder myhotels

True leadership is about being a source of inspiration to others, and to do that, you have to be inspired yourself. In LEAD! Ben's wealth of experience and wisdom shines through. He has done a wonderful job of distilling his years of working with top leaders across the planet to give you the golden nuggets you need to be truly inspired.

Nick Williams, best-selling author of eight books including *The Work We Were Born To Do*

Working with Ben Renshaw has been instrumental in building a high performance leadership team to help us deliver our new Terminal 2. In LEAD! he shares his ideas and tools which made a tangible difference to our success.

Brian Woodhead, Commercial Director Heathrow

My fuel as an entrepreneur is inspiration. It is a fundamental requirement to fulfill your potential and I welcome LEAD! as a powerful reminder about what's most important to tap into your own entrepreneurial spirit.

Simon Woodroffe, Founder Yo! Sushi

LEAD! is dedicated to my three amazing children –
India, Ziggy and Zebedee –
thank you for taking a lead in my life and making it
better than I could have ever imagined.

Acknowledgements

Leadership is about relationship, and I'm truly grateful to the wide range of partnerships that have inspired me to write *LEAD!*

It is my privilege to thank my clients, who have challenged and stretched me to deliver the best possible service:

IHG – Your great leadership and commitment to creating Great Hotels Guests Love is an inspiration. Thank you to Richard Solomons (CEO), Kirk Kinsell (President, The Americas), Tracy Robbins (Executive Vice President, Global Human Resources and Group Operations Support), Keith Barr (Chief Commercial Officer), Angela Brav (Chief Executive, Europe), Kenneth Macpherson (Chief Executive, Greater China), Eric Pearson (Chief Information Office), Jan Smits (Chief Executive, Asia, Middle East and Africa).

Heathrow – Your passion and commitment to Making Every Journey Better is outstanding. Thank you to John Holland-Kaye (CEO), Norman Boivin (COO), Emma Gilthorpe (Regulatory Director), Paula Stannett (HR Director), Phil Wilbraham (Development Director), Brian Woodhead (Commercial Director), Becky Ivers (Talent and Development Director HR), Elaine Grix (Head of Leadership).

Home Retail Group – Your dedication to leading with purpose and developing talent is admirable. Thank you to Pete Connor (Group IT Director), Julie Elder (Group HR Director) and Sian Evans (Head of Leadership).

Allen & Overy – Your willingness to grow and serve at the highest standards is nothing short of remarkable. Thank you to Tom Brown (Partner, Hong Kong), Grant Fuzi (Partner, Sydney), Genevieve Tennant (Global Director of HR).

Special thanks are due to Pierre Danon (CEO, BT Retail), Nick Cullen (Group Supply Chain Director, Clarks), Dave Woodward (Former Executive Vice President, President and CEO, Europe Heinz), Will Morris (Group MD Retail, SSE), Imelda Walsh (HR Director, Sainsbury's), Alistair Gilmour (Managing Director, Shell), Sophie Turner Laing (Managing Director, Entertainment, News & Broadcast Operations Sky). Each of your commitment to leadership development is exemplary.

My business partnerships – which have provided memorable opportunities and great support.

Dr Robert Holden, Founder of Success Intelligence & The Happiness Project – thank you for your thought leadership and inspiration. Avril Carson – thank you for your love and willingness to shine. Graham Alexander, Founder of The Alexander Partnership – thank you for your coaching brilliance and wisdom. Mike Manwaring – thank you for your dedication and friendship. Deborah Tom – thank you for your belief and high standards. Linley Watson – thank you for your vision and support. Nick Williams – thank you for your courage and simply being there.

My publishing team, who have brought out the best in me to write *LEAD!* Ed Peppitt – thank you for your infectious optimism and excellent guidance. Amanda Cohen – thank you for your outstanding editing expertise, rich insight and enduring support. Lisa Snape – for your typesetting skills. Adrian Burrows – for your design expertise.

My photographer and friend, Cambridge Jones, award-winning photographer and recently described as 'The Brits' answer to Annie Leibovitz', who has photographed four British Prime Ministers, The Queen, Al Pacino and everyone from Sir Anthony Hopkins to James Bond. Some of his recent work resides in The Queen's private Library at Windsor Castle. Thank you for your generosity and creative brilliance.

My friendships, which have constantly energised my writing along the way: Andy Thrasyvoulou – thank you for your love and inspiration, which nourishes my life. Simon Woodroffe – thank you for your creativity and passion, both totally catchy! Mike Mathieson and Martin Stapleton – thank you for our True North group that keeps fulfilling its purpose. Kelley Stapleton – thank you for your encouragement and expert eye. Debbie Oakes – thank you for your extraordinary love and support.

My family, who make it all worthwhile. My mother, Virginia – thank you for being a loving presence in my life, and for your selfless dedication and editorial support. My father, Peter – thank you for your endless encouragement and being on the same path. My sister, Sophie – thank you for being honest and staying connected. My cousins, Dave & Debbie White and Eg & Polly White – thank you for your creative ideas.

Most importantly, my wife Veronica – thank you for believing in me and fulfilling our dreams together. Thank you to our children – India, Ziggy and Zebedee for bringing love, laughter and fun into our lives.

Printed and bound in Great Britain by
CPI Group (UK) Ltd, Croydon, CR0 4YY

ISBN 978-1-907798-51-1

Certain names and other identifying details have been changed to protect the privacy of individuals. Although the author and publisher have made every effort to ensure that the information in this book was correct at press time, the author and publisher do not assume and hereby disclaim any liability to any party for any loss, damage, or disruption caused by errors or omissions, whether such errors or omissions result from negligence, accident, or any other cause.

Contents

MY LEADERSHIP MANIFESTO

Top 10 guiding principles

1. Leadership is not a position, role, title, status or paycheck.
It is a way of being and an attitude that shapes your life, work and relationships.

2. The most important aspect of leadership is to be authentic.
In other words, commit to being who you really are.

3. Great leaders have a clearly defined leadership philosophy.
What you believe about leadership guides your decision-making and behaviour.

4. The way to build credibility as a leader is by delivering on your promises.
Turn your vision into action.

5. Being in service to others is the highest form of leadership.
Service is not sacrifice – it's about understanding and meeting others' deepest needs.

6. A true leader brings out the best in others.
Enable people to go beyond what they think is possible.

7. Leadership is relationship.
The only way you can lead is to build a deep emotional connection with others.

8. In order to lead others you must keep growing yourself.
If you don't grow, others can't grow.

9. Leadership is all about the example you set.
The way to test your leadership is by valuing honest feedback.

10. Leadership is about inspiring others.
In order to inspire, you need to be inspired yourself.

Introduction

As the applause died down, I looked out into the audience.

Surrounded by the stunning backdrop of the Canadian Rockies, right in the heart of Banff, I felt a deep sense of appreciation. Having the opportunity to do what I love – and showing others how they can immeasurably transform their work and lives – is what inspires me every day.

While presenting to the senior leaders of one of the largest energy companies in the world on inspirational leadership, I realised yet again what a core issue 'inspiration' is.

Inspiration is both the essence and challenge of leadership.

The greatest contribution that you can make as a leader is to inspire others.

But in order to inspire others you need to be inspired yourself.

A major survey of up to 2,000 managers (by the Chartered Management Institute and Demos in 2001, who built on the work of the Council for Excellence in Management and Leadership) revealed that the single most important factor most people wanted to see in their leaders was inspiration.

However only 11% actually saw their leaders embody this ability. A significant gap, you'll agree. As leaders, this is a challenge we all face. We would like to believe that we light up a room when we walk into it. However, others might experience it as the room lighting up when we leave it!

LEAD! is the synthesis of my insights, based on over twenty years of coaching global leaders to be the best they can be in today's ever-changing world. And the fundamental proposition at its core? Inspiration.

In 50 easy-to-read chapters, you will find out more about such concepts as individual leadership styles, high visibility, the 'ripple effect', prioritising, 360-feedback, mindfulness and deepening trust, just to mention a few. There is advice on how to develop your physical, emotional, mental and spiritual success and how to use all aspects of your multifaceted intelligence. Written in digestible 'sound bites' you can apply it immediately.

No excuses.

I could have written 52 chapters, but wanted to give you a couple of weeks off to enjoy finding different kinds of inspiration!

But seriously, why is inspiration so important?

Think about this.

You have 1440 minutes in a day. Letting you off for sleep time, imagine what it would be like to commit to making most of those minutes truly inspiring:

When you wake up in the morning, are you on autopilot as you reach over groggily for your smart phone – or do you take a moment to truly consider the gift of a new day and how you can make the most of it?

Do you greet your loved ones with genuine appreciation – or with the routine of packing school lunches and racing out of the door to beat the traffic?

When you reach the office, do you take a few precious minutes to connect with your colleagues – or immediately power up your PC?

During the day, do you simply tick off the 'to do' list – or ask yourself, *How can I make a real difference today?*

Focusing on inspiration is a true act of leadership. It is the most significant thing you can do in your day. Truly.

You might not believe me, but getting even the most successful business leaders, entrepreneurs, educationalists, health professionals and artists I've worked with to invest a small amount of precious time to inspire themselves is a big deal.

And yet the results speak for themselves: heightened awareness, increased clarity, greater energy, smart decisions, courageous conversations and deeper fulfillment. When you think about the number of minutes that go past in your life which are simply wasted through getting caught up in mindless chatter, repetitive thoughts and unconscious habits, surely to reverse this trend can only be a good thing? Life is too short, after all.

I wrote *LEAD!* to remind us of what's most important in our crazy world, where human activity has become increasingly accelerated and our challenges even more complex.

On the one hand, geophysicist Richard Gross – based at NASA's Jet Propulsion Laboratory in Pasadena, California – reported that following the massive earthquake that struck northeast Japan in March 2011, the intense temblor accelerated the Earth's spin, shortening the length of the 24-hour day by 1.8 microseconds.

Yet on the other hand, in many economies, growth is slowing down. According to Bloomberg Businessweek global economics (April 25, 2013): *'China's growth is decelerating much faster than anticipated. Yes, the slowdown is for real;*

that's caught many economists by surprise and is fanning worries that China won't be the hoped-for engine to drive a global recovery.'

On the business side growth is also cooling. As the BBC reported (January 25, 2013) Apple lost its crown as the world's most valuable publicly traded company that same month, despite record profits, as the tech-giant had been hit by fears over its future growth.

LEAD! is your companion for thriving in this pressure cooker. Its 50 concepts are designed to inspire you to Take a Lead in your own life, work and relationships. Each chapter shouldn't take more than a few minutes to read. It doesn't matter how you read the book – dipping in or cover-to-cover – however, it does matter what you do it with it.

Don't just pay lip service. Take each idea on board. Make the book your leadership gym. You will exercise new muscles that you never even knew you had. Take the time to stretch them. Use the practical exercises at the end of each chapter, headed **Take a Lead** as mental workouts to accelerate your leadership ability.

Take this book personally.

It was written to inspire – and enable – you to be the best possible version of yourself.

Ben Renshaw, London 2014

What is your definition of leadership?

It never ceases to amaze me how most of the leaders I work with have not defined what real leadership means to them – even if it is part of their job title.

Chapter 1

Defining Leadership

John was a high flyer. A seasoned executive and number two at a global technology firm based in London, he was married with four children and enjoying life to the full. A home in Tuscany for the summer months, and winters spent skiing in Chamonix meant he could indulge his taste for fine wine. As a result of his success, John had recently been sponsored for a leadership assessment by his company in order to ascertain his suitability to progress towards becoming CEO. The subsequent report showed that he had the ability to deliver outstanding results – and that his knowledge of the industry was second to none.

The problem? His ability to inspire and engage others; in short, to lead. On the back of these findings I got a call from the company's HR Director to see if some coaching could make a difference in accelerating John's leadership development.

Ahead of meeting John I got descriptions about him. Intimidating. Imposing. Sceptical. These were the adjectives used by his colleagues. So, over two steaming coffees I took the direct approach – asking him right away how he defined leadership. John's response hit me in the gut.

'I'm not a leader,' he said, barely meeting my eyes. 'I'm a technocrat.'

Here was the root of the dilemma. Because John had not worked out what leadership meant, his ability to lead was severely limited. And this blind spot was showing itself to be a real threat to his future success.

Stop reading for a moment.

Ask yourself, *What is my definition of leadership?*

If you need some encouragement there are thousands of definitions out there. Just type in 'leadership' on Amazon. com and you'll find at least 108,911 books to select from.

Every organisation I have had the privilege of working with has their own definition. One leader at Heinz was passionate about *everyone being a leader*. He wanted his people to recognise that *who they are* and *what they do* makes a difference. The British satellite broadcasting company, Sky, defines leadership as having *head, heart and guts*. Their philosophy is to show strategic thinking, heartfelt passion and the courage of conviction. At the InterContinental Hotels Group, the largest hospitality company in the world, leadership is defined as *having purpose*. Their philosophy shows that by defining *your own core purpose* you are able to lead and inspire others.

My definition? I discovered it some years ago. But more about that later.

So, what's yours?

Without a clear definition of leadership you will not be able to truly lead.

Once you have defined it, you will be able develop your own leadership philosophy.

'Philosophy' comes from the Greek *philosophia*, which means 'love of wisdom'. I'm not saying that you should sit around and naval gaze. Far from it. Thinking about leadership is a dynamic action that demands you draw out your own wisdom on the subject. *A real leader consciously works out what leadership means.*

Back to John. Our coaching relationship gave him the time and space he needed to explore his own definition of leadership. And he found it. At the heart of it was the metaphor of an orchestral conductor. John loved music and could see that the brilliance of a conductor is needed in order to synergise and inspire his 'orchestra' which is made up of different 'specialised experts'.

This understanding changed John from being technically focused, to inspirationally orientated – a significant factor in his future successful transition to CEO.

In a nutshell, the way I define leadership is a mindset and a way of life. It is not a role, title, pay check, level or job. It is not what happens as a result of a promotion or a position of hierarchy. Real leadership is the way you grow your physical, intellectual, emotional and spiritual capability in order to inspire yourself and others.

Remember, your leadership definition lies within you and your success as a leader demands that you define it.

Take a Lead

1. What is my definition of leadership?

2. Reflect on two key questions to inform your
   response:

• *Who do I most admire as a leader, and why?*

and

• *What is the wisest lesson I've learned about
  leadership?*

Think carefully. Your answer is unique to you.

PQ, EQ, IQ, SQ

Developing your multiple intelligences enhances
your leadership.

Chapter 2

The Four Intelligences

It was 1995 and I had just finished helping organise a personal development event in London called, 'The Next Step', for the inspirational teacher Sondra Ray.

Attending was a pioneer in the world of psychology, Dr Robert Holden. We sat down for a chat over lunch. I was familiar with Robert's work from his numerous media appearances, however it was rare to come across another man who was as passionate about the sporting world as he was about transforming human behaviour. It was the start of a fifteen-year partnership which launched two visionary projects: *The Happiness Project* – following on from the BBC QED documentary, 'How to be Happy' – which gave scientific credibility to Robert's work – and the second, *Success Intelligence*, after the publication of his book by the same name (now entitled *Authentic Success*).

At the heart of *Success Intelligence* is the concept of 4 Intelligences, which led to one of the greatest revelations of my adult life – that only by developing all 4 of our innate intelligences can we fulfill our true potential.

We all know about IQ. We grew up being told that it measured our real intelligence. But in the 90s, the radical concept of *Emotional Intelligence* (EQ) was brought into the business world by Daniel Goleman, showing that defining and using one's emotional skill set was in fact a significant leadership differentiator. Then in 2000, *Spiritual Intelligence* (SQ) came onto our radar screens through the work of quantum physicist, Danah Zohar, emphasizing the need for meaning; and in the last ten years *Physical Intelligence* (PQ) has emerged as an important new player on the team.

However, it was Robert's dedication to studying each Intelligence, identifying their linkages and highlighting their distinctions, which brought them together as a unified family. His work in this area has greatly influenced my views, and work in, developing leaders. Using the 4 Intelligences is the essence of *LEAD!*, and they are the backbone of each chapter. Below is an outline of each, and a brief overview of how you can use them as focal points for your own leadership development:

PHYSICAL INTELLIGENCE

1. Energy
What energises you? Energy is what makes things happen. Energy is infectious. And it creates results. A lack of energy affects all the other intelligences: it's hard to manage your emotions (EQ), think clearly (IQ), or be inspired (SQ) when you are exhausted. As a leader, your number one responsibility is to energise others. A team that is low on energy doesn't function effectively. Clarifying and incorporating what most energises you allows you to rise above the daily grind and excel in your work and life – inspiring others to do the same.

2. Impact

What impact do you have when you walk into a room? As a leader it is essential to understand and utilise this skill. Do people *want* to engage with you, coming up to you to share ideas? Or do they make themselves invisible and wait for you to leave? People around you want to feel vitalised, and look to you for this precious commodity. Many leaders are surprised to discover that their impact entering a room, attending a meeting, or giving a presentation is not what they think. This insight can be a genuine wake-up call, and a catalyst for changing your leadership for the better.

3. Presence

How present are you? Leadership happens in the here and now, and your ability to be fully present will *define* your reputation as a leader. The most admired leaders are those able to set aside interferences and distractions and be fully present. Their presence is the strongest and most fully felt. The leaders that cause the most frustration in others are those who are unable to fully absorb the moment. Focus on the game at hand and you will be amazed at the changes that occur.

4. Well-being

How is your vitality? Are you in great health? A leader is a corporate athlete. You are required to be on top of your game at all times. However it is a marathon, not a sprint. Leadership demands that you manage yourself well, taking care of your physical needs: diet, exercise, rest, relaxation and rejuvenation in order to perform at your best, and maintain your well-being. Remember, a healthy leader is a vital one, inspiring others to reach higher and further in their own lives.

EMOTIONAL INTELLIGENCE

1. Awareness

How well do you know yourself? Self-knowledge is the gate way to great leadership. When you are able to understand yourself, your purpose, values, strengths, weaknesses, relationships, habits and skills you can influence your circumstances using your emotional intelligence. Every situation we find ourselves in allows us to increase our awareness. We do it through mindfulness, reflection, disclosure, review and feedback. Raising your awareness heightens your leadership abilities.

2. Feeling

How emotionally 'literate' are you? We have access to multiple feelings – anger, frustration, fear, happiness, excitement, love – which can be a source of great inspiration for our leadership if we are able to manage them well. Our ability to feel, understand and be responsible for our feelings is directly correlated with our ability to lead. If we have low emotional intelligence our feelings can cause havoc. Working with countless leaders has shown me time and time again that you simply don't know what is going on in someone else's life until you understand how and why they feel the way they do.

3. Connectivity

How strong are your relationships? Leadership *is* relationship, yet most of us spend most of our time focused on task. This eclipses the vital need to build the trust, empathy and respect that makes all things possible. Everyone has the potential to build great relationships; to make this a priority and allow your relationship skills to develop requires listening, working collaboratively, valuing differences and showing you care. How well do you connect with people?

4. Influence

How effective is your influence? Influence comes from understanding another's needs. It's about showing deep empathy. Investing in relationship. Once these building blocks are in place, you have the platform to influence others in the direction you want to go. A great CEO once said that the turning point in his leadership came when he realised his role had become too big for him to control everything; he had to learn to master the art of influencing.

INTELLECTUAL INTELLIGENCE

1. Think

How smart is your thinking? Most leaders find themselves too busy to think. Yet the fundamental role of a leader is to work things out – and thinking issues through is what gets you there. Your job is to enhance vision, nurture relationship, build strategies, prioritise, be accountable and communicate effectively. Mastering these challenges takes thoughtfulness. For starters, try taking just 1% of your working day – that's just 880 seconds – and spend it on quality 'think time'. Are you taking enough time out to think?

2. Clarity

How clear is the direction you are headed in? As a matter of course, leaders have to wrestle with ambiguity, uncertainty and unpredictability daily. However, you must provide clarity of purpose, direction and focus for others. This means developing the ability to make the complex simple. Clarity emerges one thought at a time, one conversation at a time and one action at a time, particularly when you face big issues. How well do you understand situations, and clarify them for others?

3. Decisiveness

Do you have a robust decision-making process? When clear, most leaders know what decision to make. It takes courage to put it into action. Making well-timed decisions is crucial. Do you have the right support in place in order to help you do this? Simon Cowell's philosophy is to make one great decision a day. If you remain true to it for a year there is no doubt that you will come up with some game-changing decisions. How can you enhance your decisiveness?

4. Alignment

Do you easily get everyone on the same page? And heading in the same direction? This is an art and a skill. It requires you to be clear about the why, what and how of your role, goal and game plan. Good leadership is a combination of your personal vision, patience, understanding and collaboration. Are these aspects sufficiently aligned *before* you move into action? Nurturing true alignment is one of the smartest investments you can make with your time and energy.

SPIRITUAL INTELLIGENCE

1. Purpose

What is your true purpose? Why do you do what you do? These are the big questions you need to ask and answer in order to lead well. You must know what you are made of, your core DNA, the essence of you, what takes you further on a higher level. In the absence of this awareness you run the risk of being inauthentic, chasing false goals, and being unfulfilled. Everyone has a purpose. It is your birthright. An essential part of your leadership journey is to discover what your true purpose is and to live it every day. Are you living your calling?

2. Values

Do you have a moral compass? Your values and moral stance tend to originate from the adversity that you have experienced in life, crossroads you've reached and dilemmas faced. Your definition of values such as integrity, honesty, resilience, responsibility, love and freedom forms the fabric of your character. It is essential in gaining the trust and respect of your colleagues. To lead with conviction requires an inside knowledge of your values, where they come from and how you live them.

3. Vision

How clear is your picture of your desired future? A leader is a visionary. I'm not talking about putting your vision on the world stage right now, but about the need to create a vision for your own physical, emotional, intellectual and spiritual future. Leaders invest time in discovering their dreams. They apply their imagination to thinking bigger and doing things differently. Are you succeeding in painting the picture only *you* can?

4. Inspiration

What truly inspires you? Inspiration is the essence of leadership, but in order to inspire others you need to be inspired yourself. Inspiration comes from countless sources – family, business, the arts, sports, leisure, history, nature, science, comedy, people, politics, religion, philosophy, creativity or service. Can you commit to recognising and cultivating what inspires you on a daily basis?

The four intelligences – PQ, EQ, IQ and SQ – require a lifetime of study. While our education places the main emphasis on IQ in determining our initial work experience, afterwards it is our PQ, EQ, and SQ which make the biggest difference to our effectiveness and development as leaders.

Start to identify which type of intelligence is at play in your work, life and relationships, and which of them need enhancing. The simple act of paying attention and being curious about how to improve these four key players in your life will increase your inherent ability to develop each one.

How are the four key players in your team doing?

Take a Lead

1. Rate my levels of intelligence on a scale of 1-5
   (1 = low, 5 = very high)

   PQ _____ EQ _____ IQ _____ SQ _____

2. How can I develop the intelligence where I
   most need it?

A clear definition of success is your compass

Without a clear definition of success you cannot truly know in what direction you are headed, whether you are on track or when you have arrived at your final destination.

Chapter 3

Define Success

Successful But Something Missing, my first book, summed up my life experience up until that point.

I had chased and achieved many goals, both on a personal and professional level – yet there was a constant hole inside me that could not be filled by achievement alone. After considerable reflection, in which I challenged myself to understand the root of what was missing, I realised that although I had worked hard to be successful, I had no true definition of the word: I hadn't yet worked out what success really meant to *me*.

This is one of the most common dilemmas that I have encountered while coaching leaders.

So, I decided to crack my definition of success. I mean, really crack it.

I made a commitment to write down the question:

What is success for me today?

and to write the answer in my journal every day for a year – 365 days – committing to answering it during the course of that day. Until then I had tended to live so far ahead of each day that I was unable to assess success in the moment. A common problem for us all!

Initially I resisted it and found myself forgetting about the assignment sometimes until half way through the day. However, like building any new muscle, the longer I continued the easier it became. My definitions of success fluctuated each day. For example:

'Inspire everyone I meet'

'Complete my to-do list'

'Enjoy today'

'Be a loving husband'

As a result of doing this I was able to look back at each day and review how I got along.

Everyone around me began to notice the difference. But no one more than myself. I felt more focused, and more free. So I took it further – from daily to yearly, projecting my definition of success into each area of my life, using a timeline: 1 year, five years, 10 years, and then my final year of life.

In order to get a balanced 'scorecard' I broke success down into these five arenas:

Physical Success	Work Success	Life Success	Family Success	Spiritual Success

I can honestly say the benefits have been amazing. By focusing on what success means to me on an annual basis, I now find that I have a clear focus for each year, which enables me to stay on track and enjoy the journey as I go. By defining success for the longer term I have developed an ability to gain a much greater sense of appreciation for, and perspective on, what is most important to me both now and in the future.

Physical Success

Take Gill. She had landed on her feet, having recently been offered her dream job in America. It was part of her rise up the company's ladder, and she began the process of relocating with her family. Gill worked in an exciting part of the business, which was central to the fast growth of the company. She powered away in her first few months, but when I eventually caught up with her there was no doubt that the pressure was taking its toll.

She was exhausted. Her sleep pattern was affected. She had stopped exercising regularly. Her diet had gone awry due to the amount of air miles she was clocking up. It was simply not sustainable.

What did she need to do to rebalance? We went right back to the basics of defining success for Gill on a physical level. She set some tangible goals about her sleep (6 hours a night minimum), exercise she enjoyed (cross-country walking and pilates) and nutrition (no fast foods) – as well as building in time for the required support to help her along the way, such as regular massage and acupuncture sessions.

The majority of people I work with are stretched – long hours, demanding work schedules and energetic children mean that you must look after your physical well-being in order to enjoy sustainable success on a physical level.

Work Success

David was becoming increasingly frustrated with his experience of success at work. He had been in his organisation for some ten years, during which time he kept seeing himself passed over, while his peers' careers progressed forwards. He was becoming increasingly disenfranchised and considered leaving the company.

Before making any major change I encouraged David to redefine what success at work meant to him, in particular to move away from seeing it as a ladder going upward. He agreed to start by exploring his definition of success in 5 years' time, which he defined by giving each year a particular theme. As you see, it includes more than just a promotion:

2014 Inspiration

⇨ I have real energy that people feel.
⇨ I convey a sense of possibility.
⇨ I am making things happen to realise my potential.
⇨ I am doing things differently.
⇨ I have think-time.
⇨ I have a strong team which is set up for success.
⇨ I have deep and strong relationships with key stakeholders.
⇨ I enjoy a bigger picture and broader perspective on life.
⇨ I have clarity on the 'why' and where' of the direction I'm headed.
⇨ My life plan is focused on doing something different.

2015 Perspective

⇨ I have a wider perspective about different cultures and ways of doing things.
⇨ I am able to engage others in conversation from their outlook.
⇨ I am opening doors for my kids to have broader perspectives.
⇨ I have a sense of personal possibilities.
⇨ I am building my reputation externally.
⇨ I am focused on delivering my business plan over a 3-year timescale.

2016 Vitality

⇨ It's all about out-performance.
⇨ My kids are happy and learning.
⇨ Being on the Executive Committee is a step away.
⇨ I am helping drive the company through to the next chapter of its evolution.
⇨ I am loving what I am doing.
⇨ I have a sense of other possibilities.
⇨ I am invigorated by what I am doing.

2017 Life

⇨ I am on the Executive Committee helping to shape the company's future.
⇨ There is a buzz – I am part of one team, sharing common values and goals.
⇨ The organisation is a great company to work for and there is recognition of my value.
⇨ I am being strategic in my approach.
⇨ I am an industry personality.
⇨ I have helped prepare the kids for their next chapter.
⇨ I have an understanding and a plan for my marriage when the kids leave home.

2018 Possibilities

⇨ The company is recognised as a great company.
⇨ It is well on track to deliver its strategic goals.
⇨ I have a hand on the tiller and a strong functioning team who are open to fearless honesty.
⇨ I am working collaboratively, joining the dots across the organisation.

⇨ I have a deep understanding of the enterprise and know the levers to pull.

⇨ I am enjoying work and life.

⇨ I enjoy regular travel through social and work.

⇨ I am proud of my kids and being part of their growth as human beings.

Remarkably, within weeks of completing this exercise David was nominated for the promotion he'd been waiting for the last couple of years. Why?

My belief is that once he had a clear definition of success deep inside, it shifted his focus from being externally led to internally driven. This resulted in him becoming a compelling candidate for succession in the organsiation.

As a consequence of this experience, David continues to fine-tune his definition of success – both in the short and long term – to ensure that it is the true compass he follows.

I have witnessed this phenomenon *over and over again*. The more people are able to define the question: 'What is success?' at work, the more opportunities open up which they could never otherwise have predicted.

Life Success

Then there's Paul. Someone who suddenly found himself at a pivotal stage of his life, heading up the marketing division for a rapidly growing company. He had very demanding targets, which required him to stretch every capacity to achieve. Married, with two children under the age of five, he was totally stressed out. One of the first conversations we had was about how he defined success in life. His response was narrow and revolved around a financial number at work.

When I asked him to think about the impact on his life were he to continue in the groove he had set, he reflected that he might achieve his number but probably wouldn't have a family to accompany him along the way. We deepened the inquiry about success in life and he arrived at an ultimate definition of success – freedom. He recognised that this was the major driving force in his life.

We explored what freedom meant to him and the image that came to mind was his favourite pastime, being a surfer riding the big waves.

Given his high drive for immediate results, he wanted to chuck everything in and move to the beach. I managed to restrain him long enough to think hard about how he could bring more freedom into his life today, rather than make any reactive decisions. I asked him to rate his level of freedom on a scale of 1-10 (10 standing for total freedom). He was at zero. I challenged him to define what moving to 1/10 would take in his life right now.

His response?

To play 10 minutes of his own music on his i-pod first thing, before starting his conferences calls in the car. This small act was symbolic to Paul, and meant putting freedom first. It started him on a journey which, several years later saw him able to buy a place by the sea where he could indulge his passion for surfing. Meanwhile, he began taking his kids to school a few times a week and made time for regular dates with his wife, so they could get to know each other again.

Once you have defined what success means to you, you are well on track for *making it happen*.

Family Success

Tom had been fast-tracked at work, resulting in him burning the candle at both ends. The major impact of this challenge lay in relation to his family. His wife was feeling the pressure of looking after the kids on her own during the week, and though he made repeated promises to get home on time, he found himself breaking them more often than not. A wake-up call hit Tom when he arrived home at 8pm one night and received a standing ovation from his family for just making it before bedtime. This was not how he wanted to live. However, whenever he tried to discuss the situation with his wife he got a frosty reception due to the fact that he had broken his promises so many times that their emotional bank account was overdrawn.

I advised Tom to confide in his manager as it was clear that he was not going to be able to resolve this on his own. Thankfully Tom's boss was very sensitive to the situation and suggested that we dedicate one of his coaching sessions to a joint session with his wife. It was a poignant session as the three of us sat down to reflect upon their marriage and family with a view to redefining success for them. What emerged was a shared desire to re-prioritise the family and get back the fun and togetherness they had had before Tom had hit the fast lane. They agreed that although the increased status and financial package that accompanied his achievements at work were valued, they were not as valuable as being a family. Together they looked at Tom's schedule to figure out how he could keep his promises to the family, and once his wife had shared her frustrations her frosty exterior melted and allowed her love to shine through. Tom realised that hours put in don't always mean productivity and with the goal of getting home on time, learned to work more effectively without putting 'company' time on 'home' time's account.

Whatever form your family takes, your ability to dig deep and define what success looks like for you and your loved ones is the place to start in order to nurture genuine family success.

Spiritual Success

Brian was a real deal maker. Renowned for his ability to close a deal, even at the expense of others, Brian had a reputation for his aggressive, transactional orientation and lack of empathy. It got him financial results, but didn't win him many friends. I was brought in to coach him as a last-ditch attempt to retain him in the organisation, since the Board had virtually lost patience with his increasingly unsavoury reputation. The message was loud and clear. Change or be changed.

My first step was to conduct a 360-feedback exercise to illustrate the impact that Brian was having on others. Overlooking the London skyline from his glass-windowed office, it was a high-pressured moment when I debriefed him on the findings. As expected, he reacted strongly to the feedback and used his performance results as evidence for the top quality work he was doing. He took the stance that if anyone disliked his approach it was their problem, not his. I reminded him that our coaching sessions were a last-ditch opportunity to help him become aware of his behaviour and make some new choices, otherwise his time in the company was limited.

After several sessions, there was very little evidence of progress and I was beginning to doubt whether the process would work.

The breakthrough came over the Christmas period. I had tasked Brian with the assignment to redefine success for *himself* over the holidays and not to come back to work until he had it figured out! A high-risk strategy.

However I will never forget the moment when I sat down with Brian again – several days into the new year. He said that he had applied himself wholeheartedly to the exercise and had arrived at three conclusions about what success meant to him:

1) *Personal growth*. He recognised that what he really wanted to focus on now was how to help others succeed. He had young kids that he wanted to nurture and help to grow, not to mention the talent around him in the company.

2) *Philanthropy*. After crunching his numbers Brian admitted that he had real financial security. It was now time to give back and help others less fortunate than himself.

3) *Spirituality*. Brian explained that he had grown up in a religious family, but had rejected it early on in life. Now he really wanted to understand what spirituality meant for him and his family.

I nearly fell off my chair. I would never have predicted such a U-turn. Having a spiritual dimension to success enabled Brian to look at his behaviour at work with new eyes. He recognised that taking an aggressive stance did not align with his real definition of success and he committed to changing his ways.

Ultimately, spiritual success comes in various different forms. It's about what inspires you and gives your world real meaning. It's about creating a vision of what *you* want to create in the future. It's about discovering and living your purpose and becoming connected with a deeper wisdom that guides your choices.

Defining success provides clarity about what is most important and how to measure what matters. It is not a one-off exercise. It is a continuous inquiry in getting clearer about what is most important to you, allowing you to stop chasing false idols.

If you don't define what success looks like to you, your life will happen – but probably not in the way you would like it to.

Take a Lead

What is your definition of:

• Physical Success:

• Work Success:

• Life Success:

• Family Success:

• Spiritual Success:

Your mindset inspires your results

Simply put, inspired choices lead to
inspired consequences.

Chapter 4

New Mindset

Upon awakening, what is on your mind? Do you hit the snooze button or is the prospect of a new day so tempting that you leap out of bed? Do you have inspired thoughts, or simply thoughts? At the start of every leadership programme I ask the participants what their initial thoughts are first thing. Their responses are truly inspirational!

A cup of coffee
Sending an e-mail
What to wear
Beating the traffic
Getting the kids up
Taking the dog out
An early meeting
The weather

It's a 'to do' list.

Important? Yes.

Inspired? No.

Occasionally I get more enlightened answers like:

Appreciating the value of life.
Loved ones.
Looking forward to the possibilities of a new day.
Making the most of the here and now.

It's interesting to note most of these responses are given in Asia where there is higher spiritual intelligence and recognition of the importance of things like values, purpose and meaning. I also hear it from those who have overcome huge adversity, and as a consequence focus on what is most precious.

It is estimated that we think approximately

50,000

thoughts per day. That's a lot of thinking. The way to clean up your act and become deliberate in your mindset is to understand three different paradigms that influence your thinking. Determinism. Choice. Intention.

Determinism

The Oxford Dictionary defines determinism as *the doctrine that all events, including human action, are ultimately determined by causes regarded as external to the will*. It's a pretty fatalistic approach which leads to conditioned reflexes.

Remember that famous experiment of Dr Pavlov's? Back in 1901, he rang a bell every time he fed his pack of dogs. They began to salivate, not paying conscious attention to the bell. He discovered that over time, by simply ringing the bell – with no food in sight – the dogs would be set off, and begin to 'dribble'. This is known as a 'conditioned reflex'. Even if we are not consciously deterministic, we have so many conditioned reflexes that often we are no different from Pavlov's dogs.

The bell of life goes off and we dribble. For instance, we have a meeting with a 'difficult' customer or client, and we already predict the angst that will accompany the experience. Our kids have a mountain of homework to do, and we brace ourselves for the inevitable fallout. We have become conditioned by our experience. We operate on autopilot and apply little conscious thought to what goes on.

Choice

Probably the biggest psychological breakthrough in the last century was the recognition that we have choices. In between stimulus and response, there is choice. *As human beings, we have the ability to choose our response in any given situation.*

The most powerful work that I've come across about choice theory is Victor Frankl's. An Austrian neurologist and psychiatrist, he survived the Holocaust after several years in some of the toughest concentration camps in Europe. Frankl was founder of 'logotherapy', which explores the will of meaning. In other words, what determines our will to survive. He noted that some men gave up and others kept the flame of life burning, even if their circumstances were identical. He realised that it was all in the mind: those who held onto what was meaningful to them – a wife, missing child, book to be written – had more chance of surviving. One of the most poignant statements he makes in his classic book, *Man's Search for Meaning* is:

'Everything can be taken from mankind but one thing: the last of the human freedoms to choose one's attitude in any given set of circumstances, to choose one's own way.'

Each and every single moment of your life you are making choices. You are choosing to read this paragraph. You choose the work you do and the organisation you work with. You choose the relationships in your life. You choose how you spend your time. Even if it doesn't always feel as though you are making deliberate choices, you are, from the deepest subconscious level to the most clear and conscious ones.

Matthew, one of the most impressive leaders I have had the privilege of coaching is a passionate advocate for the power of choice. Matthew will consistently thank his employees for choosing to work for the company. He acknowledges that they have choices and that they could be using their talents elsewhere. In meetings he will sometimes start by thanking people for attending. Many find it disconcerting as they didn't think they had a choice, especially as he had called the meeting. However Matthew reminds them that they are deliberately choosing to spend their precious time in this meeting, now, and he recognises this fact.

In order to lead you must become *consciously* aware of the choices you make.

Intention

In determining your mindset there is a one other vital factor to consider – intention. An intention is something you commit to which determines your choices and guides your actions. Intention has its own intelligence. Although you may not know *how* you will manifest an idea or solve a problem, your willingness to set a conscious intent is the place to start.

I believe all acts of inspiration start with intention. The genius of Apple had its origins in Steve Jobs, whose intention was to marry perfect technology design with creativity.

The majesty of Michelangelo's David was inspired by the great artist's intention to discover the exquisite statue inside the marble, where he believed it already existed.

Mahatma Gandhi's deepest intention was to inspire a movement of non-violence, civil rights and freedom in India, as a result of his experiences of injustice in South Africa.

Consider the idea of waking up each morning with the intention of being inspired and inspiring others? What might that lead to? Rather than being on autopilot, it would encourage you to think about what you really appreciate in your life. It could lead you to engage with your family in a more loving way. And to relate to your colleagues in a more meaningful, enjoyable way. *Maybe it would lead you to doing your best work.*

Closing the gap between letting life simply happen and consciously creating life through deliberate intention is what leadership is all about.

You lead your own life, not the other way around.

Take a Lead

1. What mindset do you most want to develop as a leader?

2. How can you set a more deliberate intention each day?

3. What would it mean to you to become conscious about your choices and intention rather than operating on autopilot?

Leadership starts with the recognition that your intent affects your life

Born. Dribble. Play. Go to school. Do exams. Go to a bigger school. Do more exams. Go to university. Do more exams. Drink. Have sex. Get a job. Get married. Work hard. Have kids. Less sex. Still drink. Retire. Have grandchildren. No sex. Still drink. Die.

Chapter 5

Intention defines Outcome

As a leader you need to deliberately focus on how your intention inspires the outcomes you achieve.

You are not at the effect of life. You contribute to the creation of your life through setting conscious intentions of how you want it to be. For instance, to realise your leadership potential you must intend to understand and demonstrate the brilliance of your unique talent. To build a high performing team, you must first intend it and then take deliberate actions to nurture and create an environment where people can perform at their best. To become a great parent, you must intend to be the best parent you can be and then continue to learn and grow every step of the way.

On a personal note, an example of how *someone else's* conscious intention has impacted my life was inspired by my marriage to Veronica, who comes from New Zealand. Little did I know that when we got together it would entail yearly December trips to New Zealand – right in the heart of an English winter – in order to rejuvenate and see her family. When she first suggested the idea, I dismissed it as 'nice but hardly realistic' due to time and work commitments.

However, she had no intention of allowing my excuses to get in the way.

Well, after one particularly grueling year in which I had been daily dominated by my to-do list, I returned from a memorable Antipodean visit only to land up back in my office in early January, to what seemed like a particularly dark, cold and wet London day. I distinctly remember that first Monday back at 'work'. I couldn't face it. Here I was. Self-employed. Nobody to be accountable to and yet I knew that I couldn't continue in the same vein that I had left a few weeks before. As I reflected on my options I took a step back from all the possible tasks I should do and asked myself, *What is my intent here?*

I realised I wanted to love what I do. To be genuinely inspired and excited by it. Keeping up my puritanical work ethic was *not* going to be the answer.

So that morning I quit. I resigned from my job. I handed in my notice… to myself. It seemed crazy and yet right. The move I made was a symbolic act to quit the work ethic that was killing my creativity. I recognised that my real passion and joy was to serve. Service to me is one of the highest forms of leadership. It is about leading with your heart and making a real difference to the lives of others.

From that moment on my intention was to serve others with passion, creativity and love – allowing me to make the biggest possible difference for others whilst flourishing myself.

And I have never looked back.

I still have times when the to-do list takes over, however I'm able to refocus myself in an instant through reminding myself of my true intention.

One way I support this process is to take my personal development journal and write down the question, 'What is my intent today?' I did this every day for a year. Some days my intent was to inspire, others it was to learn and sometimes it was to be creative. The act of doing this built my intention muscle so that it is now a habit that I simply would not want to live without.

Before you get busy starting up projects, running meetings, having conversations or taking action ask yourself, *What is my intention in this situation?* Setting a conscious intent is a powerful act of leadership. Remember, intention determines the choices you make and the actions you take. Therefore the clearer you are about your real intent, the better your outcome will be.

Let the power of intention guide and inspire your every thought, word and action.

Take a Lead

1. What is my intention today?

2. And tomorrow?

3. And the day after that?

4. How can I help my true intention clarify itself?

To Be or not To Be

Leadership is about remembering that
first and foremost we are human beings,
not human doings.

Chapter 6

Back to Being

One of the most fundamental steps to take in order to be an inspiring leader is to move from a state of 'doing' to a state of 'being'.

When your existence is dominated by a to-do list you are operating in a transactional mode. Sometimes I come across so-called leaders who describe themselves as 'doers'. This is not leadership.

Leadership requires that you have a heightened awareness of how you want to be. Shakespeare's famous line from Hamlet, *'To be or not to be'* resonates so deeply because it touches the depth of our souls about the significance of being. It would not have had the same impact had he written, *'To do or not to do'*.

Most of us adhere to the theory below:

Theory 1

Have	Do	Be

Theory 1 is based on the idea that if we *have* enough: status, achievements, contacts, money, houses, cars, handbags, we will *do* the things that we want to do: work, travel, activities in order to *be* the type of people we want to be: happy, successful, fun, inspiring, energising, loving.

Theory 2

Be	Do	Have

Theory 2 turns this around. The proposition is that instead of waiting until we have the things we think we need in order to do what we want and be the kind of person we want to be, we decide *how* we want to be first. Our state of being then shapes what we do, as well as what we have.

Nick was probably the most action-orientated and performance-focused leader I have worked with. He was the epitome of Theory 1 and would drive his team with a stick in order to fulfill their key objectives. It worked in the short term as evidenced by the results they achieved, such as delivering consistent outperformance in the marketplace. However, at a certain point in time, employee engagement levels began to drop and staff went looking for other jobs. It was at this point that Nick asked for my help.

We started by addressing his type of leadership. It was very clear that Nick had one primary operational mode – doing. I introduced him to the idea of 'being' and challenged him to recognise that unless he shifted his focus, he would soon be without a team. Nick understood the theory, however was sceptical about applying it, as he had relied on his old trusted formula for so many years.

But he wanted to make the change.

Given the challenge Nick faced – how to really engage his people – we started off by analysing how he wanted to *be* in order to increase that engagement. He understood that at the heart of engaging people is their need to be *seen*, *heard* and *recognised*. However Nick acknowledged that he rarely demonstrated behaviour that facilitated this. So I asked him how he wanted to be in order to inspire and engage his people.

He admitted that he was permanently distracted, always chasing the next goal in his action-oriented pursuit of doing, which was causing a lot of the frustration for others. 'For starters,' he said in his top-floor office, 'I would like to be more present.'

As a practical first step, he repositioned his one-to-one meetings with his direct reports as 'being time'. While still covering updates, Nick encouraged an open agenda where people could bring to the table any topic they wanted to discuss.

As a second step, Nick decided that he wanted to be inspiring to his team. He deliberately slowed down his formidable pace and started to listen to people when he walked about the office, taking time to connect and really understand what was going on. He asked his team to give him feedback when they saw him distracted, or consumed by tasks, which helped him to significantly raise his awareness about the impact of being.

Nick's shift in focus created immediate results regarding his employee engagement. Retention levels went up, thereby stemming the loss of talent. After six months he conducted a 'pulse survey' to test engagement levels. There was marked improvement with overall levels having risen by 8%; and on a grassroots level, his employees reported feeling far more appreciated for their individual contribution.

Nick's commitment to 'being' flowed into his personal life. Instead of filling up his weekends with things to do, he spoke with his family about how they could be together in ways that allowed them to enjoy each other's company more, rather than simply pass each other by. For instance, they decided 'to be present' when together, which resulted in iPads being powered down and phones set aside; and they had fun enjoying a Friday evening meal as a family.

In an organisational context, probably the most significant shift that individual contributors and managers have to make as they step up into higher leadership roles is the move from doing to being. Up until then they have been rewarded for how much they do, and how well they do it. However, leaders are ultimately remunerated for their quality of being. If we look at some popular business leaders, each of them stands out from the crowd by being unfailingly true to their innermost being, their *way* of being, and refusing to compromise it: Steve Jobs, for being innovative and creative. Bill Gates, for being a thought leader and having a philanthropic attitude. Richard Branson, for being a maverick and having a fun attitude. Mark Zuckerberg, for being entrepreneurial and connected.

The art of being is an act of intentional leadership.

Take a Lead

• How do you want to be?

• Sit with this question. Let it guide and inspire you.

• Let your 'being' inform you of your answer and then commit to it each day.

Great leaders are simply themselves

Our authentic self is the essence of who we are. It is the natural, gifted self at the core of our being, unblemished by the good or bad opinion of others.

Chapter 7

The Age of Authenticity

From the age of eight, I grew up studying violin at the prestigious Yehudi Menuhin School, nestled in Surrey's lush green countryside.

My father was headmaster there, giving him the opportunity to combine his educational vision with his passion for music, while my mother was the heart of the school and provided unconditional love for the children while teaching cello, French and Italian.

Although a talented violinist, I was not that happy there. Music was simply not the right medium for me to express my creative self. Most days I felt a pull to be somewhere else. As a consequence I learned to adapt my behaviour, becoming an excellent chameleon. I could fit into any situation we encountered – whether it was playing to elite audiences in the beautiful mountains of Gstaard at Lord Menuhin's summer festival, or performing in schools, hospitals and prisons around the country. The conscious journey of reclaiming my authentic self didn't properly begin until I left the school.

The majority of my fellow students went straight from school to music college. I was the exception, taking a gap year out to travel. I chose Israel – my destination Kibbutz Magen, a collective community situated in the Negev desert. I will never forget the moment I arrived in Tel Aviv, still wrapped in my thermals after leaving the cold of an English January, simply carrying my backpack and violin. I had a few hours in the bustling city before my bus left for the desert, so decided to wait at the beach, overlooking the Mediterranean. In that moment, looking at the cerulean sea, I experienced a tremendous sense of freedom as I pictured all my friends practising away in a music studio, whereas I was here embarking on an adventure to discover my real self.

In a Harvard *Business Review* article, 'Discovering Your Authentic Leadership' (by B. George, P. Sims, A. N. McLean and D. Mayer) the authors note:

'After analysing 3,000 pages of transcripts from leaders we were startled to see that people did not identify any universal characteristics, traits, skills, or styles that led to their success.

Rather, their leadership emerged from their life stories and understanding who they were at their core. They discovered the purpose of their leadership and learned that being authentic made them more effective.'

Being authentic can appear to be an overstatement of the obvious. *Be yourself*. However, it is not always as straightforward as it sounds. We live in a world where many of the messages we receive reinforce the idea that we should be somehow different from who we really are.

Our parents, usually with good intention, want us to conform to societal norms – either academically, socially or work-wise – in order to 'get ahead'. Our education builds upon this notion as we get squeezed through the system, which is great if you fit in, and very limiting if you don't. Our media paints a picture of what we should look like, listen to, watch, read and whom to base our role models on. All these factors can detract from our ability to know what is right for us, often with the result of people forgetting, hiding or diminishing their real strengths and talents.

As I see it, we have two selves at play – our *authentic* self and our *learned* self.

Our authentic self is the *essence* of who we are. It is the natural, gifted self at the core of our being, unblemished by the good or bad opinion of others. Our learned self is the consequence of our conditioning from a wide variety of sources including family, culture, religion, social milieu, education, media and organisational set-ups.

Take Simon, for example. Well into his 40's, and on the cusp of a promotion that would take him to new heights in his publishing company, the dream of leading a major business was in sight.

But as we sat together, contemplating what this opportunity would mean, a key obstacle surfaced.

Simon was concerned that once entrenched in the new role with its new responsibilities and targets, he would stop being able to be his authentic self. So we deepened our investigation and found that the source of this concern lay in his upbringing. Simon's parents had instilled very strong core values in him when he was growing up, in particular the importance of 'doing the right thing'. His father had had strong ethics and left jobs if he'd felt that his values were being compromised, even if it may have been financially detrimental for his family. Simon followed in his father's footsteps. Early on in his own career, he too had landed up in a couple of companies that rubbed up against his core values while he was looking for his authentic voice – and he'd moved on accordingly.

In his new role Simon would be following on from a dictatorial leader. Although this person had left people scarred by his forceful manner, he had added great value to the business. Simon questioned whether his own genuine warmth and desire to do the right thing would work once the buck stopped with him. It took a great deal of courage to risk being authentic as he stepped into the new role. He had to make some important decisions about people in his first months, replacing some colleagues who did not share his value set. This sent a loud message to the organisation about how committed he was to leading with values such as integrity and fairness.

As part of his coaching programme I conducted a 360-feedback survey to understand how a wide range of people rated his leadership. The overwhelming response? That people were truly inspired by having a leader whom they could respect. And the fact that he retained his authenticity in the new role was his winning formula.

In contrast, our learned self is a false picture of who we think we should be.

Take Clare, the top saleswoman in her company. Renowned for her brilliant abilities and delivering well above her annual targets year after year. Her manager, a great believer in the benefits of coaching (especially for his highest performers) invited me to work with Clare. In our first session Clare shared all the positive stuff that was going on, however she also revealed what kept her awake at night: the moment she had to present a financial spread-sheet to her manager each month.

This seemed highly irrational, as the numbers Clare presented were outstanding and she had a strong relationship with her manager. As we probed further, what emerged was a belief that she wasn't great at numbers and she was concerned that this would be exposed when she made her presentation. It transpired that at school Clare had been labelled 'stupid' by her Maths teacher, as a result of finding it difficult to recount her times table in front of the class. The label had stuck and now, as a highly successful adult, she still believed it. I asked if Clare knew her IQ; she didn't, and she had avoided ever finding out in case it confirmed her worst fears. As part of her commitment to resolving the issue, Clare agreed to go online and take her IQ test. Her score came out just fine.

That was Clare's first step to reduce the impact of her learned self. The next step was to share her anxieties with her manager. Luckily, he was an empathetic man who welcomed her confidences. They agreed that Clare would get feedback each month about how well she communicated the numbers during her presentations so that she could get an accurate picture of her effectiveness. This process debunked the myth of Clare's 'learned self' and allowed her to be more authentic.

Research about leadership shows that it is the ability to be authentic which distinguishes the good from the great.

Becoming an authentic leader starts with the intention to be authentic. *Yes*, it's a risk. Yes, some people might find it challenging as they start letting their real selves come through. However, there is nothing as soul destroying as being dominated by your learned self and losing the brilliance of the real you.

Take a Lead

1. When am I being most authentic?

2. How do I behave when I'm being myself?

3. What are the benefits?

4. When am I being least authentic?

5. What is the impact of not being myself?

6. How can I be more of my real self?

Know Yourself

Building on the concept of our learned self comes the
opportunity to understand our personality type.

Chapter 8

Personality Types

I used to be a professional worrier. Anxiety ran my life.

If I caught myself not worrying, I worried about why I wasn't worrying. I thrived on Woody Allen's neurotic humour and loved his line: *'Most of the time I have no fun. The rest of the time I have no fun at all!'* It wasn't until I started to learn about my personality that I could relate to myself in a different way, and realise that anxiety did not have to define who I was.

Today there are many personality profiling tools, all of which are useful for heightening self-awareness, accelerating personal growth and deepening compassion for others. Of everything I've come across, the Enneagram has had the profoundest effect on my life.

Coming from the Greek *Ennea* (nine) and *grammos* (something written or drawn) the Enneagram has its origins in the work of Evagrius Ponticus, a Christian mystic who lived in 4th century Alexandria. George Gurdjieff, an Armenian philosopher, is credited with introducing the Enneagram to the West in the early 1900's, and in the early 1960's two psychologists, Oscar Ichazo and Claudio Naranjo developed it into the form we know today.

The Enneagram model explores nine interconnected personality types. Don Riso and Ross Hudson, founders of the Enneagram Institute in America and authors of numerous books on the subject, are two of the most remarkable teachers I have come across.

They were introduced to me by Robert Holden, founder of the innovative *The Happiness Project* and *Success Intelligence* which we co-directed. My work partner for fifteen years and a good friend, Robert knew me well and took his time mentioning the concept. I initially resisted his suggestion that I take a break from my busy schedule to find out more – however after observing the profound impact it was having on his own life, I decided to go to America and learn about the Enneagram for myself.

The rewards were immeasurable. Basically, the Enneagram system helps you understand your best, essential self. It shows how you behave under pressure – when your personality (the familiar conditioned part of yourself) reveals itself most clearly. Using the model, you will find yourself identifying with one dominant personality type – your inner, inborn temperament, if you like – which determines the ways in which you learnt to adapt to your early childhood environment and which continues to influence your behaviour. That is, until you develop enough awareness to recognise what you are doing, and decide to make new choices.

The following is a simple, but accurate thumb sketch of the 9 basic personality types, giving the essentials of each, the typical behaviours to watch out for (red flags) and some coaching tips. Out of respect for their groundbreaking work, I have used Don and Russ's naming of the Types. As you read through the descriptions, see which you most identify with:

Type 1 – The Reformer

The essence of Type 1 is being a catalyst for possibility. Reformers have a passion for creating tangible changes and love seeing things improve. They embody a strong sense of responsibility and advocate high standards. At their best, they have great wisdom, a natural vision and the capacity to make important decisions based on a broad outlook.

Red flag: Being overly critical evaluators, Reformers have a tendency to criticise others, which can leave them demotivated and unclear about solutions. Coming across as cynical and dismissive, their desire for perfection means that they set unrealistic standards neither they nor anyone else can meet. They take on too much due to their overly developed sense of responsibility, leaving themselves exhausted and irritable.

Coaching tips: Become clear about your personal purpose, which will inspire and sustain you during times of change. Discover how to really enjoy the successes in your life in order to become more light-hearted about what you are aspiring to achieve; and learn to give recognition to others' efforts by energising and inspiring them.

Type 2 – The Helper

The essence of Type 2 is pure love. Helpers have an open-heart, possess great empathy and enjoy the ability to nurture others and help them grow. At their best, their love is a unifying force based on an unselfish desire to make the world a better and more loving place. They embody natural generosity, and are a true friend to others.

Red flag: Slipping into self-sacrifice, Helpers find it hard to take the lead as they are such good supporters of others. They struggle to distinguish their own needs as they become overly focused on others, leaving them in a vulnerable place as they neglect their own feelings and get lost in trying to please others. One of their biggest challenges – loving to give, they keep an 'account' and when they don't believe that they are receiving back on equal terms, give with strings attached.

Coaching tips: Be emotionally honest about what is going on. Watch out that positivity does not act as a cover for more difficult feelings. It's important for you to understand and meet your own needs in order to avoid descending into self-sacrifice. Discover what you really love and commit to letting love guide your choices.

Type 3 – The Achiever

The essence of Type 3 is to inspire others to be the best they can be. Achievers have a great ability to see the big picture, focus on results and manifest new possibilities. At their best, they are authentic role models for how to lead a truly successful and inspired life, and have the courage to serve real causes which make a genuine difference in the world.

Red flag: Self-deception. Achievers can get lost in their own self-image, believing they are coming across as sincere when at times the opposite is true. They have to be the 'special one', the centre of attention, and find it very difficult to let others shine. They can be controlling, feeling that 'their way is the right way'. This results in excessive individualism and burn-out as it is impossible to succeed on one's own.

Coaching tips: Take sufficient time to redefine success so that you become very clear about what is most important, rather than striving for outward goals. Understand what success is from your heart and soul – as well as your head. It is also essential to identify when you are being truly authentic and to recognise how you can be more so in relationships in order for others to really connect with who you are.

Type 4 – The Individualist

The essence of Type 4 is to be highly creative in an authentic way. Individualists have a great ability to be emotionally honest, which inspires others to be their authentic selves. At their best, they are able to translate experiences, including difficult ones, with acceptance and insight, thereby transforming them into meaningful events; they are extremely talented when it comes to creating beauty, and often make their mark in memorable ways.

Red flag: Shutting down emotionally and withdrawing. Going into their own world, Individualists may fail to communicate with others as to what is going on, and what their real needs are. Although their personality requires emotional intensity, when this is taken to extremes they become moody and difficult to be around. Humour goes out of the window and one feels as if one is treading on eggshells, hoping not to get on their wrong side.

Coaching tips: Ensure that you have enough time and space to connect with what is most meaningful in your life. Keep in close touch with your individual talents and strengths in order to enjoy authentic achievements. It's very important to be around people who bring lightness and humour into a situation, so that you can be drawn out of any melancholy and prevent life from becoming a drama.

Type 5 – The Investigator

The essence of Type 5 is a deep knowledge and understanding of any given subject. Investigators have an innate ability to develop complex ideas and skills, and become the expert in every situation. At their best they are visionary leaders, and able to see things in new and different ways; they have genuine curiosity to learn, explore and gain fresh insight.

Red flag: Overthinking. Investigators get stuck waiting for the ideal conditions in which to act and often end up blaming others for their failure to put ideas into practice. Due to their high intellect they tell themselves that they know it all, become closed-minded and shut down to other perspectives and ways of looking at things. Their mind is so filled with thoughts and theories that they can forget to connect with others, losing touch with the outside world.

Coaching tips: Engage in physical activity to blend with your mental activity, ensuring a healthy balance. You need to cultivate a rich social life and stay connected with others, which will help prevent becoming reclusive. Meditation is a valuable practice for Investigators, as it allows your mind to relax and rejuvenate.

Type 6 – The Loyalist

The essence of Type 6 is to enable others, helping people to do their best in their lives. Loyalists are highly conscientious, making sure that everything is as it should be and working to optimum capacity – whether it's in a relationship, a process or an organisation. At their best, they provide a bedrock of support both for themselves and others to act with courage, take risks and follow their authentic vision.

Red flag: Worrying about anything and everything. Often plagued by self-doubt, causing them to question their own judgment, they turn to others for answers. Unfortunately they may then resent the sources of authority that they have relied upon and turn against the very supporters who have championed them. This is the result of a lack of basic trust in the world, caused by a sense of suspicion about the motives and intentions of others.

Coaching tips: Define a vision for success based on your own inner wisdom. It's essential that you are clear on what is right for you, rather than being overly influenced by other people's point of view. As a Loyalist you must learn to ruthlessly prioritise what is most important in order to prevent yourself from becoming too stretched. It's also vital that you stay inspired by enjoying what nourishes and sustains you.

Type 7 – The Enthusiast

The essence of Type 7 is to be the life and soul of the party. Enthusiasts possess tremendous energy and optimism, which lifts other people's spirits. They have a natural capacity for seeing new possibilities and ways of doing things. At their best, they focus their talents on meaningful goals and apply a practical approach to getting things done. They are highly productive and can spread themselves across multiple projects with positive results.

Red flag: Being bored. Their low interest threshold means that they move on fast, often too fast, before something has been given sufficient thought. They tend to be very reactive, as they thrive on spontaneity, however this can cause chaos and others being left exhausted, in their wake.

Coaching tips: Learn how to focus and organise yourself. You will see that being more organised liberates you and ensures that others can understand the direction in which you are heading. It's very beneficial for Enthusiasts to slow down in order to make space for more creativity and imagination. If you are running too fast you tend to get lost in the blur of your own life. It's helpful to remember John Lennon's famous quote, *'Life is what happens to you while you're busy making other plans'.*

Type 8 – The Challenger

The essence of Type 8 is being a natural born leader. Challengers have great strength and power which acts as a galvanising force. Decisive, they are always up for a challenge, and love to take the initiative. At their best they help create a strong vision and will champion a strategy to create winning results. They have big hearts and will support others in being the best they can be. Living in the present, they are always prepared to take significant action in order to raise the game.

Red flag: Becoming overly challenging and verging on aggressive behaviour. Challengers can undo a lot of their good work through forcing others against their will, and coming across as too hard or intimidating. They can be too controlling, stifling the innovation and creativity of others.

Coaching tips: Get regular feedback from trusted sources to understand how you come across, paying particular attention to dominating or forceful behaviour. Allow others to support you wholeheartedly, thereby establishing powerful partnerships and preventing you from becoming overly independent. It is also helpful to work out clear measures of success to ensure you don't constantly strive for success but feel that you never arrive.

Type 9 – The Peacemaker

The essence of Type 9 is to bring great clarity and calm to the world. Peacemakers trust the natural process of creation, thereby living with a sense of wholeness and harmony. At their best, they are able to bring others together, acting as mediators and facilitators. They are accepting and able to live in the here and now. They look for the best in all situations and want the highest good for everyone.

Red flag: Living life on the sidelines. Peacemakers become passengers rather than pilots, and let others dictate the way forward. They will try and avoid conflict at any cost; however, unresolved feelings tend to get suppressed and can then rise up in unhelpful ways. They don't like to be the centre of attention, so will repress their own personal needs in order to accommodate others. However if and when they do assert their needs people take affront as they are surprised by it. Peacemakers will often daydream as a way of avoiding their personal reality, which perpetuates the tendency to become disengaged from life.

Coaching tips: Find ways to ground yourself and be present, such as physical exercise, engaging in projects and organising events. You need to set clear action plans with realistic timelines and get somebody to hold you accountable to delivering on your promises. It's essential to stop trying to please everyone in order to keep the peace. Doing this can actually lead to more conflict, as it encourages emotional dishonesty.

The purpose of understanding personality typologies is to heighten your own self-awareness in order to gain greater clarity about your behaviour patterns, and thereby your true identity; as overly identifying with your personality can severely limit your ability to inspire and engage others. Remember, having a sense of other people's personality type is extremely valuable too, as it helps you tap into deeper levels of compassion and understanding for them.

Self-knowledge is the gateway to great leadership.

Take a Lead

1. Write down 3 adjectives that describe you at your best:

- _____

- _____

- _____

2. Write down 3 adjectives that describe you at your worst:

- _____

- _____

- _____

3. Reflect upon which personality type you identify with and how your descriptions support your observations.

If you don't go within, you will go without

All great leaders I have worked with have a highly developed sense of intuition which enables them to be clear in their decision making, read social dynamics and stay true to a course of action even when it requires some tough moves.

Chapter 9

The Inner Game

Pete, simply one of the most remarkable leaders I have ever come across, was responsible for several thousand people in the engineering sector, and renowned in the industry for his innovative approach.

His thought process is several years ahead of most people, and he comes across as considered, clear and consistent. Under pressure, he rises to the challenges he finds on his plate; and on the home front enjoys a humble lifestyle with his tight-knit family and his love of the outdoors.

I was intrigued by Pete's formula for such genuine success, so I invited him to present at one of my advanced leadership programmes for a group of high potential leaders. His title, *Inner Leadership*, immediately captured my imagination. I knew we were in for something special.

At the appointed hour, Pete showed up with a golf club in one hand and a mug of hot coffee in the other. Looking extremely relaxed, he started off by finding out from each person in the room where they were on their leadership journey and what was keeping them awake at night. It was the start of an inspirational two hours as he shared his own story, whilst managing to address each concern that had been raised.

At the heart of Pete's approach is the concept of inner leadership. Earlier in life, having been geared to follow a professional golf career, he had advanced from his caddying days up to an enviously high handicap. However, as any good golfer knows, the hardest game is the one you play between your own two ears – the game in your head!

One day, running late for a flight, Pete described how he had felt a strong pull to enter the airport bookstore before boarding. As he quickly scanned the best-seller section, his eyes alit on the title: *The Inner Game of Tennis* by Timothy Gallwey. Although not his game, something spoke to Pete, so he grabbed the book and bought it. A couple of hours into the flight, he knew why he had been compelled to enter the store. The *Inner Game of Tennis* is the classic guide to the mental side of peak performance. The fundamental hypothesis in the book is:

'Every game is composed of two parts, an outer game and an inner game: the outer game is fought against an opponent; the inner game is played against your own inner doubts and fears.'

Pete related the concept of the inner game to leadership.

Every act as a leader requires you to face the outer game – inspiring others – and the inner game – resolving your own dilemmas. The way he learned to manage the inner game was through the practice of contemplation. Pete made himself take 15 minutes out each morning to listen to his own inner thought processes in order to identify his intuition – that deepest wisdom – which gave him the conviction to act.

Intuition comes from the Latin word '*intueri*' meaning 'to look inside'. I attended a course with the renowned psychologist Gail Ferguson, author of *Cracking the Intuition*

Code. Her extensive research shows that *'intuition is a natural conductor of reliable information.'* She believes everyone can be taught to develop their intuition. *'If you know how to control this system, the bonus is that you expand your base of natural information, and can move about in your worldly surroundings more confidently and successfully than you ever could without it.'*

Ask yourself: How can I access my inner leadership? Do I allow myself sufficient time and space for contemplation and to listen to my intuitive wisdom?

Through practice you will recognise your intuition as being characterised by a sense of inner knowing and calm.

Take a Lead

Schedule 5 minutes contemplation time each morning to start listening to your intuitive voice. Focus on a particular issue that you're facing and ask yourself:

1. How would my intuition lead in this situation?

2. What would it have me do?

3. What would it have me say?

4. And to whom?

Is Man simply a knackered Ape?

One of the most vital contributions a leader can make is to energise others.

Chapter 10

What Energises You?

Are you the type of leader that lights up a room when you walk in… or when you walk out? In other words, what energy do you generate when you show up?

As a leader, it is vital to know the impact of your presence. And it all boils down to energy. As Albert Einstein famously said: *'Everything is energy and that's all there is to it. Match the frequency of the reality you want and you cannot help but get that reality. This is not philosophy. This is physics.'*

We've all had the experience of being around leaders who energise us. It's inspiring, it's infectious and we want more of it. Equally, we've been in the presence of those so-called leaders who drain us by exhibiting behaviour such as negativity, constant complaining and excessive criticism.

The challenge, however, is to know what energises you – thereby enabling you to energise others.

Laura is one the most vital leaders I have had the opportunity to coach. As Managing Director of an up-market retail company, mother of three lively kids and introverted by nature, Laura has to be mindful of how she expends her energy.

She starts each day with aerobic exercises to keep her body in great shape. She also makes sure to nourish herself with a balanced diet, being both mindful and disciplined about what she eats and drinks. Although she has a very challenging agenda, Laura works hard with her PA to ensure that she has sufficient time and space each day to draw breath, reflect and focus on what's most important. On the home front, she spends most of her available time with her family and refuses to spend time with people that zap her energy. It works. People love to be around her. Even bumping into her in the corridor is an energising experience.

I believe there are three states of being that impact on our energy:

Creative

Transactional

and

Exhausted

Creative

In the creative state, we are fully present in the here and now. We sense a heightened awareness of the importance of making the most of every moment. Even simply having the *intent* to be creative energises us. We think creatively. We engage in creative conversations. We approach situations in new and different ways. We tap into our imagination and give it free rein.

Transactional

In the transactional state, the to-do list has taken over. We are dominated by task, glued to our smart phone and caught up in activities that don't support our purpose. We are drained at the end of the day rather than fulfilled. We believe that life has to be endured rather than enjoyed. Success is simply getting through the day, rather than flourishing in the process.

Exhausted

In the exhausted state, we are on the verge of burnout. As the nutritionist Patrick Holford noted recently, *'Man is a knackered ape.'* We run on adrenaline. We live on artificial substances to keep us going like caffeine and sugar. These low-grade fuels do not support our well-being and mean that we become susceptible to illness. In the exhausted state there is a tendency to override any signals of burnout and we can end up pushing ourselves even harder in the name of success. This is not clever. A client in his 40's confessed to being on the verge of burnout when upon hearing of the death of a close family friend, his first response to his wife was, *'I hope the funeral won't clash with the meetings I've just scheduled.'*

In order to sustain your energy and nourish your creative state you need to identify these two vital questions: *What energises me?* and *What drains me?*

Some years ago I recognised that I was close to chronic exhaustion as a result of combining extensive travel, three young kids, a heavy workload and lack of sleep. I reached a point where I was simply fed up with being so tired and overstretched.

I thought deeply about where I get my energy from and what blocks it, and started by focusing on the basic ingredients for good energy such as healthy exercise, good nutrition and enough sleep. I then shifted my routine to include daily cycling, running and yoga workouts, and improved my diet by cutting out sugar and fitting quick, rejuvenating 20-minute power naps into my day when I could. I reviewed my schedule and made more time and space for researching, thinking and writing about the topics I love.

In terms of the energy drain in my life, I recognised that there were two main causes: 1 – doing things that I wasn't passionate about, and 2 – being around people who sucked me dry.

So, first I committed to weeding out any unnecessary activity that clogged up my day. I got my PA to give me 'tough love' regarding where I spent my time, and shifted to spending approximately 80% of my focus on really meaningful priorities.

It was tougher doing the same thing with people, as it meant confronting some unresolved relationship issues from the past; however I proceeded to let go of the relationships that didn't energise me and became clearer as to what relationships I wanted to sustain and nourish.

Energy is life – by increasing your own, you are able to energise others.

Take a Lead

Where do you get your energy from and what drains it?

* _____

* _____

* _____

To ensure that you are in the creative state 80% of the time, make some tangible commitments about how you can sustain your energy. I commit to:

* _____

* _____

* _____

See and be Seen

How much thought do you give to your visibility and the impact it has on others?

Chapter 11

High Visibility

A profound way of looking at visible leadership is through the lens of the South African Zulu culture.

Their daily greeting – equivalent of 'Hello, how are you?' – is *Sawubona*, which literally means, 'I see you'. The response: *Ngikhona*, meaning 'I am here'. This greeting declares that the other person is visible, and consequently is not a spirit. It embodies the concept that by recognising another you bring them into existence. It is a relational based philosophy and puts mutual respect at the heart of being with people.

I worked in an organisation where the CEO, demonstrating visible leadership, became known for his 'leader's walk'. This manifested itself in two ways: first, he advocated the importance of being deliberate about how one walks into a room, down a corridor, or in his case around an office; and second, by modelling his theory wherever he went.

On one occasion, after an inspirational presentation he had given to a group of senior leaders, he found himself running late for his next appointment. However, it was noted that upon leaving the venue – rather than rushing to his waiting car – the CEO paused for 60 seconds in the lobby, just long enough to give an opportunity to anyone wanting to say a final word before his departure. He knew very well that in taking that extra minute to be both visible and approachable he was sending out a very strong message: that he cared passionately about his people. A small moment that had huge impact.

His visible leadership can be seen in direct contrast to another CEO, who was renowned for getting to the office at the crack of dawn, heading up the back stairs, shutting his door and not coming out unless it was absolutely necessary. He was invisible. As a consequence people felt unseen, and resorted to creating their own versions of the truth about him. Safe to say, the gossip around the coffee machines and water coolers was not the stuff that legends are made of!

However, change is always possible. Coaching a sales and marketing leadership team who were focusing on improving their performance, I was also working simultaneously with their department head. So when his name came up when dealing with the team, I pricked up my ears. They were reluctant to give out much information, however I insisted, as I knew it would be valuable for their development together.

What transpired was that their manager sat on the left-hand side of the building, while they were situated on the right-hand side – furthest from the corridor and kitchen facilities. So, during the day, whenever the leader went to a meeting or popped into the kitchen to make a coffee, he would walk down his side of the office and engage with people around him. As a consequence, the sales and marketing leadership team who sat on the other side of the building felt neglected, second-best and interpreted his behaviour as uncaring since he never came over to them.

I challenged them on their 'reality' and asked if they had checked it out with their manager. They hadn't, so one of their key actions was to take steps to engage him as to their observations, and enquire about his perspective. Naturally, he had been totally unaware of the impact of his actions, and was able to explain that it was simply a matter of convenience. However he clearly recognised the effect it was having and made every effort from then on to vary his route when walking about the office.

Every moment you spend as a leader is a moment to show up.

'Elevator behaviour' is a classic example of how visible leadership can be put to the test. A pharmaceutical organisation I worked with had their head office on the 27th floor. Part of the company's folklore centred around how leaders behaved and would connect in the elevator. There was one admired leader who would always make a point of engaging people in conversation on his way up, and the more floors the elevator stopped at the better, as people genuinely enjoyed being in his presence. He knew everyone's name, he knew about their work achievements and their home scenarios.

Contrast this with another management figure who kept his head down and glued to his Blackberry, both on the way up and on the way down. It caused employees to avoid the elevator he stepped into, as it was such an uncomfortable encounter. It is no surprise that these behaviours were indicative of the performance achieved in the workplace. The admired leader had the highest employee engagement scores in the company: he attracted top talent, had the strongest customer relationships and delivered the most consistently significant financial results. Alternately, after 18 months the leader who was unable to connect with others was asked to leave the business, and subsequently found a role that demanded very little interaction with others.

I was touched by the story of one MD, who became renowned for her packet of biscuits!

It was an engineering environment with a tough shop floor and a reputation for disliking senior management. Then along came Margaret. A fearless leader, and fully aware of the dynamic at play, she scheduled an hour a day to go walkabout on the shop floor.

Initially, colleagues walked off in the opposite direction. However, after several weeks of consistent presence, people became curious about their new leader, and Margaret was finally able to start having conversations with her employees. She quickly came to understand their distrust of the 'guys upstairs', which gave her the means to address the situation. She also learned that although colleagues had access to tea and coffee, there were no biscuits on site. From that moment on, Margaret carried her own packet of biscuits with her. It was a real door opener. People increasingly responded to her willingness to be visible, and made a genuine effort to talk about the issues at hand.

Being visible is a sign of how comfortable you are in your own skin. It demonstrates how considered you are about the way you come across and the impact that you have. The power of small acts to send out big messages never ceases to amaze me. Communicating by e-mail is not enough. Sitting behind a glass door is not enough. Having back-to-back meetings is not enough. It is essential to work out the ways that you can be visible – whether it's having an open-door policy, walking the floors, giving 'town hall' meetings, holding impromptu briefings or using creative social media channels which help bring your leadership to life. Being visible shows you care. It makes your leadership credible. As Woody Allen so famously said: *'80% of success is showing up.'*

One of the most significant responsibilities you have as a leader is to be seen.

Take a Lead

1. How visible are you as a leader?

2. Get feedback from trusted sources about the level of visibility you offer.

3. Select three ways that you can become more visible and commit to following them:

- _____

- _____

- _____

Are you the pebble
or the pond?

The effect you have means the difference

between success or failure.

Chapter 12

The Ripple Effect

Leadership starts with the knowledge that you have an effect on the world around you.

The way you show up, the attitude you have, the choices you make and the actions you take all determine the effect you have. Like it or not, you have an effect on others and the situations around you 100% of the time. Ask yourself:

What effect do I want to have?

And then:

What effect am I having?

Recognise that everything you do causes a ripple – and if there is a gap between your desired effect and the effect you are having, then do something about it.

James had recently been promoted to lead a team of people who had previously been his peers. He was very concerned about the effect this move would have on his former colleagues, and how they would accept him as their new leader. His line manager was empathetic to the situation and encouraged him to work with me in order to clarify the effect that he wanted to have, and to understand what he would need to do to achieve it.

In our coaching sessions together James recognised that the main effect he wanted to have on his new team was to inspire possibility. He wanted to drive business performance and help his team grow personally. This was a big stretch for him because up until that point he had been primarily focused on delivering operational excellence. James's concern was validated when I collected feedback from his new team about their expectations of his leadership. One of the main themes expressed was the belief that he would drive the business too hard at the expense of people and that there would be casualties along the way.

James decided to step right out of his comfort zone, bring his team together and face these concerns upfront. We scheduled a two-day offsite for the whole team, in order to work towards clarifying the expectations about James's leadership and agree on the journey ahead. The entire first morning was devoted to James laying out his new leadership philosophy: sharing with his team where he had come from, what had driven him in the past, and his vision for the future. He made it very clear that he would require their full support in order to make the necessary transition. This session initiated the process of James establishing the effect he wanted to have. He was open, honest, vulnerable and humble. The team warmed to his approach, felt inspired by his intent and committed to supporting him succeed.

The effect you have makes the difference between success and failure.

Most people are unaware of the effect they want to have. They attend meetings without giving sufficient thought to why they have been invited and what contribution they'd like to make. They send e-mails without being mindful of the potential implication of their message. They have conversations without imagining how they may make someone feel.

I once received a text on a Friday evening from a senior leader requesting that we talk. I was reluctant to break into my family time, however it appeared urgent so I called him. What transpired was that just as he was heading home for the weekend, he received a call from his CEO about a meeting they'd had earlier that day. The CEO said that the meeting had not been the leader's finest hour, and that he could have done a lot more to get his point of view across. The leader was frustrated by these remarks having been made after the event rather than post-meeting, when he could have been debriefed far more constructively in person.

I suggested that the CEO was probably unaware of the effect he'd had, and that the leader should pick up with him on the Monday morning to check it out. But as he was a driven character, he contacted the CEO over the weekend, asking him how seriously he should take his feedback.

What transpired?

The CEO said he could hardly remember what he'd said over the phone, and that he certainly didn't have strong feelings about it. However he did say that he was tired when they had spoken which is probably why the remark came out in the off-hand way it did.

Not clever.

People leave jobs, demoralise teams, ruin relationships and fail to deliver results as a consequence of their inability to create the effect they want to have.

Creating the effect you want to have starts with being very clear about what it is. For instance, if you want to inspire others then you need to work out what this will look, sound and feel like. If you want to energise those around you need to understand exactly how to go about it. If you want to create the effect of helping others deliver great results, you need to clarify what part you will play to achieve it.

The discipline of asking yourself, *What effect do I want to have?* can be applied to long-term scenarios, such as defining your leadership development, contributing to organisational vision and building authentic relationships. It can also be applied to immediate situations such as running a meeting, writing an e-mail, making a presentation or holding a one-to-one review.

The beauty of the question is that it invites you to be conscious about how you come across, so that you don't just function on auto-pilot but can tap into your innate leadership ability – *to influence outcomes through a deliberate desire.* You must then follow up by getting regular feedback to ensure that the effect you are having is consistent with your intention, and if not, find out what you need to do differently.

Take a Lead

1. Ask yourself: what effect do I want to have?

Apply it when you wake up, before attending meetings, ahead of sending e-mails, prior to having conversations, before sending a tweet, and before getting home at the end of a day.

2. Then ask yourself: what effect am I having?

Request feedback from trusted colleagues, friends and family to see if your effect was the one you intended.

Carpe Diem

I used to believe that only once I'd set my life in order,
would I start flourishing in the here and now.

Chapter 13

NOW

There is a magical scene in the movie, *Dead Poets Society* when Robin Williams, playing the part of a new school-teacher, introduces himself to his class – a group of rather cynical students.

Taking them into a room devoted to former school heroes, he tells them how, for all their achievements, they are now underground and simply worm fodder. His resounding message is: *'You and me, all of us are going to die. So make it matter. Carpe Diem! Seize the day! Make your lives extraordinary.'*

This is the gift which life offers us all the time. We can either rise to the challenge of NOW and make it memorable, or let it go past in a moment of mediocrity.

Great leaders thrive on making the most of each moment in order to maximise opportunities. They have the ability to see the possible in the impossible. They have a 'can do' attitude, which inspires others to stop procrastinating and helps them to be fully present and able to face whatever challenges are before them. One of the most contagious qualities of a leader is to make the most of *now*.

So what are you waiting for? What are you putting off? What are you delaying? What are you procrastinating about?

I used to believe that once I'd got round to setting my life in order, only then I would be able to start flourishing in the here and now:

When I left school... when I dropped music... when I discovered my real purpose... when I bought my first property... when I found the woman of my dreams... when I wrote my first book... when I had enough money... when I had kids... when I got rid of the kids!

I could have gone on and on, until I finally challenged myself to lead NOW and stop waiting for some mythical time in a fantasised future.

I once coached a senior executive in his mid-forties who was successful in his role – and unhappy. When I asked him how he envisaged happiness, his response hit me like a sledgehammer.

'Retirement.'

He genuinely believed that surviving another twenty-four more years of misery would finally bring him the life he had been waiting for.

Can you imagine living so far ahead of each day that you fail to make the most of now? Consider at the age of 65 or 70, a whole life having just gone by! Crazy, and yet the majority of people do it.

Look at these classic examples of how so many leaders fail to apply the lead *Now* principle:

- I'll commit to being a better team player, *once team spirit improves.*
- I'll come up with all those new ideas, *once I have time to think.*
- I'll make better decisions, *once others come up with better ideas.*

- I'll commit to being a better leader, *once I see my senior executives model better leadership.*
- I'll get a better work-life balance, *once I win back some more time.*

And in the meantime we wait and suffer the consequences of not taking a lead now. This includes:

- *Constant criticizing*: it's far easier to sit back and judge others than have the courage to take the risk of leading NOW.
- *Ongoing dissatisfaction*: nothing is ever good enough, hence we're not able to appreciate the beauty of NOW.
- *Seeking drama*: we blow up little incidents around us, which distract us from the perfection of NOW.
- *Feeling disconnected*: we fail to feel the possibility of NOW and think we don't know enough to act.
- *Chronic anxiety*: we worry that if we simply make the most of NOW then we're going to get caught out in the future.
- *Permanent distraction*: our inability to exist in the NOW means that we concern ourselves with trivia to avoid the big stuff.
- *Being frustrated*: we find ourselves getting irritated and judgmental of others for their apparent inability to lead in the NOW.
- *Lethargy*: constantly delaying the immediacy of NOW is exhausting.

I was delighted to discover in Isaac Walther's riveting account of Steve Jobs that one of the most influential books Jobs had read was *Be Here Now* by Ram Dass. A mind-altering classic spiritual text, I came across it while working as a counselor on a summer camp in the beautiful woods of New Hampshire back in the 80s. Ram Dass, a former Harvard professor, arrived at the conclusion that the most important spiritual truth is:

> *To*
> *Simply*
> *Be*
> *Here,*
> *Now.*

What does this mean in practice?

Firstly, having a heightened awareness of when you are present and when you are not. My research indicates that we are present only about 50% of the time, the rest of the time we're caught up in past or future thinking.

Secondly, having an increased commitment to be in the NOW and to constantly challenge yourself whenever you catch yourself putting something off for a 'better time'. On occasion this might be completely appropriate, however notice if it becomes an excuse not to be present.

Thirdly, taking action NOW. One of the most distinguishing features of great leaders is an ability to act. Whether it's making a decision, rolling up your sleeves up for a task, having that difficult conversation or kicking off a project… acting NOW will take you in the direction you want to head.

The truth is that the more we give to NOW, the more we get from NOW.

Take a Lead

On a scale of 1-10 how often do you lead NOW?
(10 represents all the time)

1. List 3 ways you fail to lead NOW:

- _____

- _____

- _____

2. List 3 ways you will lead NOW going forward:

- _____

- _____

- _____

Overflowing inboxes. Twitter, Instagram and Facebook accounts. Calls to make. Meetings to attend. A never ending to-do list.

We live in a world of constant distraction. Within this state of interruption, how present are you? I mean, really present?

Chapter 14

Being Present

Of all the qualities to master as a leader, being present is possibly the most important. The bottom line is that if you are not present you will not be attuned to what's going on. You will not be able to make the right calls. You will fail to show sufficient empathy. You will come across as disengaged and distracted. You will lose credibility.

Are you able to be fully focused and attentive in the moment?

Being present gives you the license to influence others because it shows how much you care. Being present sends the message that what you are currently engaged in is of the utmost importance. Being present requires and inspires others to be present.

Take a guess as to who comes up in my leadership programmes as the most admired leader in recent history.

Bill Clinton, former US President.

Here's why.

Everyone who nominated him describes one outstanding quality he embodied... (and forget the politics or sex scandal): his remarkable ability to be present. Those who had the honour of meeting him all say the same thing. In a room of thousands, he makes you feel unique. Even if it is for just 60 seconds, he is completely there, focused. On one occasion, at the close of a conference where Clinton had been the main speaker, the host spontaneously asked him if he would be willing to walk the line. This had not been on the itinerary and it was a long line! His security guards froze. However, Clinton said 'yes' and he spent the next 40 minutes personally greeting everyone as if nothing else mattered in that moment. Was he born like that? I don't think so. Being present is an art, which everyone can learn – and practise.

The ability to be present starts by having a heightened awareness of each moment.

Do you leave your smart phone on vibrate so as not to miss a piece of the action? Are you typing up every note on your iPad to feel more efficient? Do you check your e-mails obsessively and answer your phone no matter when and where it rings? Are you constantly thinking about the next place you need to be?

As you begin to recognise how present you are – or not, as the case may be – it will encourage you to consciously decide whether you *want* to become more present. Because unless you commit to being fully present, no amount of encouragement will help. Once you've determined your appetite, you must then identify the key distractions that take you away from your goal. One leader I coached described the profound experience of becoming noticeably more present simply by switching off his e-mail programme when working on his computer. The simple act of not knowing how much e-mail traffic was going on had a measurable difference to his ability to truly address the job at hand.

In the workplace, one of the most effective ways for a leader to become present is to request feedback. Explain your commitment to being present to trusted colleagues and ask them to notice when you are really 'there' and when you are not, how your behaviour presents itself, and the effect it has on others.

One leader I coached prided himself on being totally present for his team. However he had a real blind spot during meetings. Although he'd asked his team members to refrain from checking their e-mails during their gatherings, he himself had his iPad on, quite oblivious to the impact it was having. It wasn't until we had a team development session that people were able to share the tension it caused as a result of his lack of awareness. E-mailing had become such an ingrained habit that he genuinely believed others saw his behaviour as acceptable. Once he stopped, he realised his mistake in thinking that he could clear his inbox at the same time as being present for others.

On the home front, children have the uncanny knack of demanding your attention until you become fully present. One father called this 'carpet time'. He recognised that once he came home after work it was not until he got down on the floor with his kids to play that he was able to give them the real focus they required. Another father learned to leave his briefcase in his car when he arrived home every evening, so that when he got in the house it wasn't pulling his attention away from being present with his family.

There is no doubt that when you are present you connect with what's going on around you. When you are present you connect with where other people are. When you are present you have the presence to lead.

Remember, when you are paying attention you are in the moment that's called your life.

Take a Lead

1. Assess yourself on a scale of 1-10 as to how present you are right now (10 represents being fully present)

a) In your home life:

b) At work:

c) Socially:

If you score less than an 8, ask yourself, *What would need to happen in order to become more present?*

Repeat this process until being present becomes a habitual way of being.

What is Your Purpose?

I believe we are each born with an innate purpose.

Chapter 15

Lead with Purpose

The InterContinental Hotels Group (IHG) is a global hospitality company with nine brands, spanning 4,700 hotels in nearly 100 territories and countries.

Their guests book more than 160 million stays per year.

Several years ago, IHG went through a transformative process led by their former CEO, and supported by their Executive Committee. Their groundbreaking decision? To adopt an asset-light business model and sell the majority of their hotels.

This meant moving from being a property-led company to a service-led one. As part of their journey they redefined what the company stood for, and the role they wanted it to play. They engaged with thousands of their employees throughout the organisation, seeking to discover the core purpose of the company – and concluded that their true raison d'etre was to create *Great Hotels Guests Love*.

IHG's Executive HR Director, Tracy Robbins, recognised that in order for the company to become genuinely purpose-led, senior leaders would need to understand what this meant in terms of their own leadership, as well as discovering their own *personal* purpose.

I was introduced to the company through my partnership with Graham Alexander. Graham is credited with having originated business coaching in Europe back in the early 1970's and has acted as my mentor over the years. It has been a privilege to partner with IHG as a major client, and together with my colleague Mike Manwaring, we developed a senior leadership programme for the InterContinental Hotel Group, called 'Leading with Purpose'.

Over the last 7 years we have trained hundreds of IHG leaders from around the world. It has been a life-changing experience, supporting leaders in America, Asia-Australasia, Middle-East, India, China and Europe as they discover their own personal purpose and understand how to best inspire and engage others through being purpose-led.

As the current CEO, Richard Solomons recently testified:

> *'Leading with Purpose has supported the*
> *career journey of many of the strong*
> *leaders that we have in IHG today.*
> *The reason is its unusual focus for our leaders*
> *on why they do what they do and how they*
> *use that knowledge to motivate and inspire others.*
> *I encourage all those at IHG who*
> *aspire to senior leadership to participate in*
> *the programme if they genuinely want to*
> *maximise their potential.'*

We are each born with an innate purpose. I believe that the process of discovering our purpose is an internal one and involves uncovering what already exists within us. We do not have to manufacture or make up a purpose. But the journey of exploration takes a genuine willingness and honesty to allow the light of awareness to reveal our true purpose.

Having a core purpose is the reason for our existence. Our individual purpose is based on a deep conviction about what is most important and precious to us. It inspires possibility. It shapes our attitudes, guides our choices and determines our destiny. A purpose has a timeless quality, which goes beyond the circumstances of our lives and provides a true compass for us to follow. There is nothing more powerful than knowing what our purpose is… and then living it.

In the 'Leading with Purpose' programme we use the following exercise to define purpose. It is the most profound tool I have used in over twenty years of developing leaders. You'll need to find a quite spot and set aside around 60 minutes to complete it:

Step 1

Create a lifeline by drawing a horizontal line across a page. This represents the duration of your life to date.

Step 2

Below the line, chronologically mark the key experiences and turning points in your life, noting the impact of each event, what you have learnt, how it has shaped you and what conclusions you have drawn as a consequence.

Step 3

Reflect upon how each experience has informed your values, i.e. the beliefs you hold that are most important to you.

Step 4

Look at your list of values and select 3-5 core ones.

Step 5

Above the line, mark peak moments in your life – for example, when you have been most fulfilled, at your best, in flow and inspired.

Step 6

Make links between these peak moments and use the following questions to define your purpose:

- What is the key contribution I want to make?
- Why do I do what I do?
- What is most meaningful in my life?
- What is the difference I want to make?
- What is the legacy I want to leave?
- What do I want to be known for?
- What is my joy?
- What truly inspires me?
- What am I most passionate about?
- What do I love?

I'm often asked, *How will I know my purpose?* Some of the key indicators include:

When I am at my best
Knowing what difference I want to make in the world
Being clear about why I do what I do
What I want to be known for
Following my joy
Being passionate
Doing what I love
Feeling inspired

There is an important distinction to make here – between your core purpose and personal values. My research indicates that a *purpose* is something we are born with. It is innate, existing within our DNA and, once discovered, changeless. On the other hand, our *values* come from learned experiences and can be influenced over time according to the situations we face.

From the thousands of experiences I have had supporting leaders in discovering their true purpose, there are certain common themes that come through. A purpose usually has to do with others, for example how to help or enable them. It has an inspirational quality to it, such as love, success, being the best, freedom, fulfillment. It is clear and simple.

Examples of purpose statements are:

- Inspiring people to go beyond what they think is possible.
- Being the best version of myself in order to inspire others to be the best they can be.
- Being a creator of opportunity.
- Helping others succeed and fulfill their dreams.
- To love and be loved.

Some examples of purpose statements from well-known public figures include:

'Live your best life' Oprah Winfrey

'Make a dent in the universe' Steve Jobs

'May all beings be happy' Dalai Lama

'The respect for individual rights is an integral part of human existence' Nelson Mandela

On a personal note my purpose is, *'To be the presence of truth.'* When I peel back the layers of my life it has been consumed with a passion for discovering the truth about any situation. I do not define what is true. However, I do create environments for truth to reveal itself.

Every coaching conversation, team event and leadership programme I run is an opportunity for people to get closer to the truth of who they are and what they are about. As a father, what I want above all else for my children is for them to know and follow their own truth, however they define it. In my marriage, I commit to the truth of our partnership to be made manifest so that we can both flourish. And I let truth guide my friendships so that they can be authentic and enjoyable.

What is your purpose? I look forward to hearing.

Take a Lead

Set aside a quiet hour to complete your lifeline.

• Key experiences

_____

_____

• Core values

_____

_____

• Personal purpose

_____

_____

Once you have a first version of your key experiences, values and purpose ask a trusted friend, coach, or advisor to share it with you to support your clarification. Request that they challenge you on your observations so that you can go deeper into your inquiry.

What are your values?

Values are the currency of leadership.

Chapter 16

Living your Values

Imagine this scene: you are alone in a rowing boat. It is filled with heavy rocks. Each rock represents a value, something that is important to you in your life, such as:

love

freedom

integrity

security

happiness

The boat is sinking with the weight of the rocks. The only way that you can stay afloat is to throw some of the rocks overboard. With each rock you choose to throw, you have to decide what value you're going to let go of, until you are left with a final one.

This is your deal breaker.

Values are the invisible currency of our lives: in our families, businesses, organisations and communities. They determine the choices we make as to what is most precious to us. People tend to choose to work for leaders with resonating values. Equally, most people leave organisations due to a clash in values with their superiors.

As a leader it's vital that you have real clarity about the values you stand for and ensure that your behaviour is consistent with them. If not, you run a high risk of having constant people issues caused by your failure to be congruent with what you espouse.

Alistair inherited a team as a result of a recent promotion to lead a larger department. He was highly principled leader, and passionate about what he believed in – he 'lived' his values. In short, his conversations were full of the need to be transparent, authentic, responsible and accountable. And he didn't just talk the talk.

In his new role Alistair quickly realised that one or two of his most senior leaders did not demonstrate the values that he cherished. He entered into long conversations with them to understand *their* values and to see if they were willing to accept those on which *his* leadership was based. He made it very clear that he was not prepared to compromise on his values; they were his lifeblood.

He gave his senior leaders the choice to either adapt to these values, or move on. It was a risky strategy as it meant potentially losing some of his most talented functional experts. However he knew that unless they were prepared to demonstrate his values it would inhibit the team from performing at its optimum level.

He found himself most challenged by one team member who had built up his own empire within the company, and was simply paying lip service to Alistair. Let's call him Bob. The trouble was that the business believed Bob to be indispensible, given his industry knowledge and expertise.

Alistair knew that this was a very real threat to his strength as a leader, and a potential deal breaker. But would the company have the guts to stick with Alistair's value-led approach?

Taking the bull by the horns he opened the subject with his boss, putting forward his case – that it was vital to follow his values in order for the business to grow and succeed. Understanding the importance of the issue Alistair's boss gave him the vote of confidence to act, and Alistair was able to manage the team member out of the business. It was a turning point for the team, as they realised the high level of Alistair's integrity; and it resulted in new levels of trust being established which became the foundation for their future success.

Contrast this scenario with Susan, who had a strong set of values too. She valued creativity, autonomy, honesty, enjoyment and love. Susan worked for a boss who made out that he espoused a similar set of values, but in fact he behaved in a very different manner. He would micro-manage her projects, check how long she'd logged on for when working from home and nod his head at her suggestions for improvements, yet do nothing about them. At first, Susan asked her boss for advice on what she could do differently in order to move things forward. To her face he would say everything was fine and that there was no cause for concern. After several attempts at trying to reconcile their different value systems, Susan realised it was time to move on.

In the previous chapter, 'Leading with Purpose', I mentioned that our values have their roots in learned experience. If you did the lifeline exercise you will already have made the connection between the most significant events in your life and how they shaped your values. Here's an example.

Rob, a leader I coached, realised that his core values were based on his early life experience. He was four years old when his younger brother was born. Being very attached to his mother, the arrival of a younger brother left him feeling deprived of her love. The consequence was that Rob landed up as an angry child with a great sense of separation from his mother. Realising the power of love, he came to value it highly.

As a teenager, Rob found himself taking risks. Once, he saw a leather jacket which he really wanted but couldn't afford. Against his better judgment, he managed to slip out of the store with it. Although he got away with the theft, he was so wracked with guilt that he forced himself to go back the next day and return the jacket. From this experience he came to value the importance of integrity.

Later on, doing well in his career, Rob was promoted to the board of the company he'd been with for some time. When he happened on a behind-the-scenes attempt to oust the founder of the business, Rob was determined the action wouldn't succeed and informed the founder. It meant taking a firm stand against his colleagues, who were driving the scheme. He found that justice was another core value.

On a personal note, I can see very clearly why I value love, freedom and creativity at a core level, and relate to Rob's story. I grew up in a very loving home. When I was eight years old, we moved from our idyllic nuclear family set-up to live in Surrey at the Yehudi Menuhin music school, where my father was to be headmaster. Suddenly, I had to share my parents' love with fifty other children. I distinctly remember the feeling that the focused love I was accustomed to had diluted – and this led to my belief in the importance of love.

Although I was a talented violinist, I knew from fairly early on that it wasn't my ultimate passion. I felt trapped in the music world, which didn't allow me the freedom to express my true calling. The decision to leave music came easily

– once I discovered the world of psychology and personal development, which was clearly my vocation. I was able to be myself and to be fully self-expressive, which for me was true freedom. I would read countless personal development books, and a seed was planted in my mind about writing my own book one day. I remember facing considerable inner turmoil due to a lack of belief in my own ability, but I was fortunate to have a very supportive editor in Judith Kendra at Random House who gave me great encouragement to follow my creative flow, and seven books later I am passionate about the value of creativity.

What are your core values? Which of them is most precious to you? Get clear on your values and then commit to living them every day.

Remember: a deal breaker is a non-negotiable value in your work, life and relationships.

Take a Lead

Make sure you have:

1. Completed your lifeline

2. Identified your values, and

3. Clarified how you can live more true to your values.

Your natural talent is your core strength

What were you born to do? What are you great at?

What do you really love?

Chapter 17

Play to your Strengths

Gallup scientists have been studying the topic of leadership over the past several decades: collating data on more than a million work teams, conducting over 20,000 in-depth interviews with leaders, and interviewing up to 10,000 employees around the globe – asking them *why* they followed the most important leader in their life.

One of their most significant findings?

That these chosen leaders knew, and played to, their individual strengths.

One of the most exceptional leaders I've had the privilege to coach is Peter. Peter's great strength lies in his ability to make connections with others.

Peter can bring people and deals together in a way that has made him a master of his profession. However, it's simply second nature to him. He doesn't have to think consciously about it. For example, when most of us would be exhausted by a demanding travel schedule, back-to-back meetings and social calendar, Peter thrives. He is positively energised by being in constant touch with the people who make up his world. He is able to create remarkable opportunities, and his big heart and attentiveness leave a lasting impression on others.

The following coaching exercise is one I use to help people identify their core strengths.

Draw up a table with two columns. On the left-hand side, note the key successes in your life so far; in other words what you are most proud of. On the right-hand side, reflect upon those qualities, characteristics and talents that you showed in order to create your success.

Here's a client's example:

Success	Quality/characteristic/ talent
Nurturing and developing free-thinking, creative, loving kids.	Empathy. Sensitivity. Care. Trust. Playfulness.
Outperforming in the marketplace for six years consecutively.	Energising others. Being bold in responsibilities. Positive impatience.
Running the London marathon in under 3 hrs.	Determination. Focus. Resilience. Energy.
Developing a high-performing executive team.	Staying focused on the big picture. Straight talking. Honesty. Fun.

The next step?

Look at the qualities that you have identified and make links and connections between them. My client arrived at three essential strengths: caring passionately for people; having boundless energy to make things happen; and a deep resilience to overcoming obstacles. He could see that pursuing these strengths created outstanding results.

However, it's also important to recognise when you *over*play your strengths, in other words when you put too much emphasis on them. This can cause you to derail.

For instance, this client noticed how his boundless energy could leave others in his wake. He would literally burn people out, as they didn't have the same capacity to keep up with his relentless pace. His passionate care could turn into a tendency to control – given how much he wanted people to succeed, it could cloud his ability to step back and let them work and develop in their own way. His deep resilience meant that at times he would over-extend himself and his self-perception as Superman, not always accurate, could leave him exhausted.

Once you've identified your core strengths you can then work out how best to integrate them into your work, life and relationships.

From a personal perspective I would say that my core strengths are authenticity, wisdom and courage.

I do my best work when each of these qualities is at play. For example, when I run a leadership programme letting my real self come through, sharing my wisdom and challenging others to be courageous in their thinking, I am able to deliver extraordinary outcomes. My relationships thrive when I'm being open and honest, and by following my courage, I'm able to maximise the opportunities in life.

Your natural talent is a core strength. It is what you are great at; it's what you love and when you express it, yields great results. There is nothing more impressive than seeing others playing to their strengths. When Rory McIlroy became number 1 golf player in the world, one of the quotes about him that particularly resonated came from fellow Irishman and three-time major winner, Padraig Harrington, who said: *'He has a good balance in his life and doesn't look like a guy who is going to burn out; he looks like he's going to be here for a while.'* Not burning out whilst being the best in the world is a great indicator of your innate brilliance.

As a young musician at The Yehudi Menuhin School in the 1980's, I watched some extraordinary strengths being nurtured and developed.

We were privileged to host the only two Chinese students studying in the West. Both just eight years old, they played great works such as the Mendelsohn and Beethoven violin concertos in a way that most of us would only dream of. They played effortlessly. The violin would slip under their chin as if they were born with it, and they became at one with their instrument. They also had a maturity beyond their years, and upon returning to China were able to build upon their musical strengths, inspiring others as they performed and taught.

Our education system traditionally develops us into all rounders, often putting greater emphasis on boosting weaknesses rather than nurturing strengths. This is reinforced in companies where once leaders reach a certain level they are expected to cover such a wide skill-set that it's hard for them to play to their strengths.

It's time to redress the balance and ensure that you lead with your strengths, in order to fulfill your unique potential.

Take a Lead

Discover your own strengths by completing the exercise in this chapter and conduct a strengths audit by reviewing how much you are playing to your strengths in your work, life and relationships.

Discover your strengths:

Success	Quality/characteristic/talent
1.	
2.	
3.	
4.	
5.	

Conduct a strengths audit by reviewing how much you are playing to your strengths in your, life and relationships.

Strength	Work	Life	Relationships
1.			
2.			
3.			

There is only one person responsible for your life

As you make the shift to real leadership, there will be no return to how you used to be.

Chapter 18

Shifting Up

What Got You Here Won't Get You There is the brilliant title by leadership guru, Marshall Goldsmith. Simply put, in order to move forward you can't trust the old formula that got you where you are today. You need a new take.

To make the shift into genuine leadership requires the willingness to understand that you are responsible for your own life.

Easy to say, right?

But far tougher to do.

We human beings have a natural tendency to want to avoid ultimate responsibility. In fact it never ceases to amaze me how people – even at a senior level – will try to wriggle out of their responsibilities. When something goes wrong, rather than owning it and getting on with fixing the problem, they are only too quick to abdicate responsibility and pretend they had no real involvement.

Remember that classic phrase in Chapter 1: *I'm not a leader, I'm a technocrat*? I have witnessed this syndrome with virtually every person I have coached during the transitional period from one leadership position to another. In that case, the words were John's, a senior leader responsible for several thousand people. There was no doubt that he was brilliant at what he did, however as he advanced to a new role, with new and different requirements, there was simply no way that he could succeed by staying put, caught up in the technology he was accustomed to. A shift was required in both his mindset and behaviour, and it took an intensive feedback process, involving his new line manager, peers and direct reports in order to convince him of the merits of shifting his leadership stance.

The key message John received from those around him was to make people his number one priority, rather than focusing on strategic planning and creating new technology platforms – especially as there were now others on board better equipped to handle those aspects. He needed to inspire and engage, coach and develop in order to build a winning team. After some initial resistance, he embraced the shift that was needed and went on to flourish in his role.

So where are you not fully embracing leadership? What shift do you need to make?

I believe there are 3 key steps to making a fundamental shift, which will propel you in the right direction:

1. Awareness

It is essential to recognise that what has caused you to succeed in the past may actually cause you to fail in the future. Ask yourself, *Am I set up to lead in my current reality?* If not, it's time to make a shift.

2. Belief

Often the shift we need to make is on the deeper level of what we believe. By holding on to a set of outdated beliefs, we can become stuck in our perception of leadership. We must examine and challenge our belief system to see if it still holds up.

For example, believing that *leadership is for a chosen few* will stop you embracing your own leadership and empowering others. Believing that *leadership is a lonely position* will stop you from reaching out to fully engage with others. *You* hold the key to unlocking your beliefs by creating new ones that will set you up for success.

3. Choice

The willingness to embrace new ideas and do things differently is essential. A small example, but symbolic: I had a favourite pair of Paul Smith shoes. I wore them daily, and they were enormously comfortable. I resisted getting a new pair for as long as I could, until finally the soles got beyond repair. I reluctantly went to replace them, only to find the line had been discontinued. Reluctantly I chose a different pair – which I found uncomfortable at first. However, I got used to them quite quickly, and soon wondered why it had ever been an issue. Every shift we make – no matter how small – is a choice to see with fresh eyes, take new steps and grow into our future.

Everyone is a leader.

Dave Woodward, former President of Heinz UK&I, wrote: *'Successful leaders have the capability to make a big difference in an organisation... and leadership is about EVERYONE.'* He also originated *'Game Changing Leadership'*, the largest leadership initiative in the history of Heinz in the UK&I, which focused on developing 1,000 managers. At the start of the programme, the majority of people attending did not have the word 'leader' in their title and had never considered leadership as part of their role. However, Dave and his executive team knew that in order to continue to succeed as a business in an increasingly competitive and turbulent climate, it was essential for everyone to tap into their leadership potential.

For three years, I ran a leadership programme together with Robert Holden, where we focused on these 3 key elements:

1 – Leading Self
2 – Leading Others
3 – Leading the Business

The resultant success stories we heard were extraordinary, as people shifted on both the personal and professional front. One manager took the initiative to engage the company in a cost-saving procedure regarding packaging, which he had identified for several years but never felt sufficiently empowered to do anything about. Within months, his product line was saving approximately £700,000 per year through implementing a leaner process. On a personal level, employees started exercising again, taking their kids to school and reigniting their marriages as they applied the essence of the programme to make change happen, rather than wait for it.

Consider making the shifts:

From	To
Role	Authenticity
Position	Contribution
Status	Value
Doing	Being
Getting	Giving
Transaction	Service
Individualistic	Collaborative
Task	Vision

As you make the shift to real leadership there will be no return to how you used to be. Recognise that your outdated model served you well once, but will not create the future you want.

Take a Lead

Apply 3 steps in order to shift your leadership on a daily basis. When faced with opportunities ask yourself:

• Am I set up to lead in my current reality?

• What new belief do I need to embrace to make a genuine leadership shift?

• What do I need to do more, less, or differently in order to shift forwards?

Yes, there is a difference

A great source of confusion in organisations
is failing to understand the difference
between management and leadership.

Chapter 19

From Manager to Leader

Great management is essential to run a great company.

The ability to be efficient, set clear targets, monitor performance and create appropriate systems are all vital ingredients for it. But management skills will be a limitation rather than a strength in the absence of such crucial leadership qualities as setting vision, creating meaning, inspiring others and driving growth.

Chris is a good example of someone who became fixated on management. He had progressed in his career by being a diligent manager and performing routine tasks with immaculate care. He was brilliant at the detail – setting up process and procedures and telling people what to do.

But as soon as the question of leadership came around? He ducked it.

Although Chris had leadership in his title, his belief was that his key role was to deliver projects on time and below budget, rather than having to step forward as a genuine leader. He hung onto his preference for management until I shared the following model with him, outlining the differences between management and leadership:

Management	Leadership
Controlling and checking	Creating possibility
Ensuring compliance	Inspiring commitment
Providing constraints	Generating options
Knowing the answer	Being open-minded
Focusing on the 'how' and 'when'	Focusing on the 'why' and 'what'
Doing things right	Doing the right things

As soon as Chris saw these distinctions in black-and-white, it opened up his mind to new possibilities. He began to make the shift towards providing outstanding leadership *alongside* effective management, realising that if he were to continue over-indexing on management it would have a serious impact on the engagement levels of the team he led. In charge of over 80 people, this was something he simply could not afford.

His own manager wanted him to get out more, increase his profile and build stronger relationships with customers, but if Chris stayed in the management box he would never have the capacity to do that. He recognised that management was his comfort zone. The idea of leadership threatened him, as it required him to develop new skills such as thinking ahead, being a storyteller, trusting in the ability of others and delegating what he'd previously done himself.

Chris pulled his leadership team together, and outlined his initial thinking about the journey he needed to undertake in order to move from manager to leader.

They listened intently to his proposition and thanked him for his awareness and courage to make the changes necessary that would help everyone progress. It was not a straightforward transition. Chris had several bouts of anxiety based on his desire to control everything, at which point he would dive into detail again by firing off e-mails to get his hands on as much information as possible. Thankfully he had a loyal and supportive HR partner, from whom he got direct feedback as soon as she saw him slipping back into the familiar old habits – meaning that he didn't slip for long.

It took about nine months for Chris to make a truly fundamental shift. He had: 1) redefined his role by putting leadership first and 2) empowered his team by having clear expectations of them and giving them concrete indications of how he wanted them to step up. At the end of the year, he found the confirmation he needed regarding his increased effectiveness, when not only his customer ratings shot up but his employee engagement scores did too.

I see the shift from manager to leader as a profound realisation for people. It is like coming of age when you realise that in order to succeed you have to face the fact that your old winning formulas could cause you to fail in the future – and that what's required is to increase your repertoire of skills to incorporate new behaviours, in order to inspire and engage others.

I am not placing a value judgment on management.

It is essential to have the ability to manage effectively; but if you want to increase your sphere of influence, you won't be able to do it whilst immersed in task. You will need to lift up and see that the future belongs to those who dare to lead.

Take a Lead

Ask yourself:

- *Is my preference to manage or to lead?*

- *What behaviours do I demonstrate as a manager? As a leader?*

If you predominantly see yourself as a manager, reflect upon what shift you need to make in order to manage effectively and lead brilliantly.

What is holding you back?

A leader's ability to welcome conflict is a sign of strength.

Chapter 20

Unblock

One thing all leaders have in common is that they are human, and part of the human condition is that we have internal blocks. This chapter will challenge you to look at – and overcome – nine common blocks which may be preventing you from fulfilling your true leadership potential:

1. Blame

Recently, I received a text from a member of a senior leadership team about an important meeting he had just attended. It read: *Excellent meeting. Anna wasn't grumpy!* Anna, the team leader, is a true visionary whose team love to follow her. With the ability to make a real difference by providing clarity about what the real priorities are, she challenges her team to deliver to stretching targets. However, when Anna is under pressure she has the unfortunate tendency to blame her team in such a way that takes the wind out of their sails. Being a leader means taking the blame *out* of situations. Real leaders take accountability for what goes on around them and quickly look for solutions, rather than point fingers. Blame is futile. It gets you nowhere, fast.

2. Drama

When the recession hit hard in September 2008, companies had to make big decisions. One organisation I worked with performed a remarkable job: while having to lay off over 20% of their senior employees, they still managed to strengthen the morale and commitment of existing employees and deliver increased customer satisfaction. What caught my attention the most? Their ability to navigate the avalanche of potential catastrophe with the least amount of drama. They provided clear and transparent messaging every step of the way. *They treated everyone with the utmost respect.* For people who rely on emotional drama, the absence of it can feel like a void. The shift required is to recognise that it's possible to be emotionally honest without indulging in drama. This results in the establishment of deeper trust and empathy all round.

3. Self–sacrifice

Do you have a habit of looking out for others at the expense of yourself? This is not genuine leadership. Rick, a good example of this, took pride in 'being there' for his people. He went out of his way to ensure that others had what they needed in order to perform at their best. He spent hour upon hour listening, problem solving and even shouldering extra tasks in order to help. However, at the end of the day he was swamped and unable to perform at his required level within the company. His big learning curve was to understand that *helping others to help themselves* was the biggest difference he could make as a leader. Weaning yourself off self-sacrifice can feel selfish at first, but as you develop the ability to meet your own needs you will be in a far more resourceful place, enabling you to read situations with a clearer perspective and ultimately allow you to add greater value as a true leader.

4. Your image

Do you need to look good? Protect your own self-image? I once coached a top team whose leader needed to come across as flawless in every situation. On one occasion, at an internal Town Hall presentation, the leader asked a question about the financial numbers in the company. However, one of the team quickly spotted that he had mis-worded the question, and therefore there was no answer. He leaned over to inform his leader of the slip, however was waved away and the leader posed the question again. Not clever. The leader's desire to look good rather than have a mistake inadvertently made pointed out worked against him. It's a self-defeating scenario because the ability to admit mistakes, ask for help and show appropriate vulnerability are all great strengths in a true leader.

5. Isolation

You know the old adage, *'It's lonely at the top'*? I certainly witness the dynamic time and time again that the more senior you are in an organisation the more political your relationships are likely to be. But instead of retreating into your own world, this requires you to become more skillful at navigating them. Isolation tends to arise out of a difficulty in relating to others, and can lead to shutting them out. I know one CEO who really struggles to connect with his people. It's almost painful watching him walk about the office, head down, avoiding contact. When he sits down for lunch, people literally move away in order not to have to endure the discomfort of being around him spiralling his isolation. Learning how to reach out and connect with others is an indication of genuine leadership, and shows that by opening your heart you can get the job done. It can start with simple eye contact, or just a hello.

6. Anxiety

You know that you suffer from unreasonable anxiety when you catch yourself worrying 24/7. The type of anxiety I'm talking about is not the consequence of an actual crisis. It is the presence of an undercurrent that clouds perception and alters reality. I coached a leader, Andrew, who suffered from high anxiety – it manifested most before having one-to-one meetings with his CEO. The anxiety was completely irrational as the CEO had recently given Andrew a sizeable promotion, and clearly had great faith in him. However, this was interpreted as more pressure, which compounded the anxiety. Our coaching focused on learning how to distinguish reality: when Andrew could acknowledge the factual basis of his position, his anxiety levels dropped and he was able to see the truth of the situation. With this in mind I then encouraged him to get candid feedback from his CEO in each of their one-to-one meetings regarding his performance in order to test if his anxieties were based on fact or fiction. Over time he came to trust the assurances that his CEO gave him, and when he did receive feedback about doing things differently, he was able to see it in perspective. The trouble with anxiety is that it only creates more anxiety. If you do suffer from it, learn to see it as a warning light on a dashboard. It is a sign that you need to pay attention to a deeper truth which lies underneath, which once discovered, will set you free.

7. Chaos

Although we live in an increasingly complex and multifaceted world, there is a difference between thriving in an ever-changing landscape, and living in a chaotic state. For those who seem to get their kicks out of a chaotic environment, things such as systems and process give the illusion of taking away their freedom and initiative. The trouble is that operating in chaos prevents them from being able to integrate in wider circles or contributing at their optimum level. Sam was a key player in a dynamic team. His leader relied on him heavily for his enthusiasm and ideas. However, in order for Sam to progress it was essential for him to embrace the working practices of the team. Each month, Sam would resist the templates laid down to create sufficient alignment in the team, thereby ensuring a chaotic status quo. The shift came only when he finally embraced the challenging concept that creativity and freedom can exist within a framework, and that his ability to demonstrate consistency would allow others to work more closely and effectively with him.

8. Stubbornness

I once coached a leader who was as smart as he was stubborn. His brilliance shone through when he had to galvanise his organisation towards a new vision. But his stubbornness would kick in as soon as he felt his opinion was being challenged, even if an alternative point of view was clearly beneficial to a project. The trouble with stubborn leaders is that they push others away, limit creative options, reduce collaboration and ultimately cause increasing breakdown of the process as people become wary of engaging with them. These leaders need to learn how to signal to people when their stubbornness kicks in, and take the time to mull things over in order to shift their position in a constructive way. They need to ask themselves, *Would I rather take an inflexible position, or allow others to help me come up with a better solution?* The only rational response is to learn to soften, and let the power of partnership lead the way.

9. Conflict avoidance

I worked as coach for a matrix team that was made up of functional leaders from across the organisation. It was brought together to deliver a high profile, complex programme and required outstanding teamwork in order to succeed. One of the most experienced leaders on the team probably had the best insight of anyone as to how to drive the programme forward. The problem? He was conflict-averse and shied away from confronting situations, which was reducing the team's effectiveness. I conducted a feedback process, whereby each member of the team had to be courageous enough to tell the others what they valued about working together, and alternately, what they'd like to see the other person doing differently. It was only when this leader received the unanimous request from everyone to embrace conflict and challenge team members constructively, that he was able to break through his limiting behaviour. I have often come across people who pride themselves on the fact that they don't have conflict in relationships. It's nothing to be proud of. Conflict avoidance is a weak position that reduces honesty, blocks energy and limits the creative process. A leader's ability to welcome conflict as part of the required growth of an individual, team or organisation is a sign of maturity and strength.

It's part of the human condition to have blocks, but a genuine act of leadership is to overcome them as soon as you recognise them.

Take a Lead

Ask yourself, *What is the most limiting behaviour I demonstrate?*

1. Identify your primary block.

2. What solutions will overcome this block?

Leadership is an act of love

When you connect with your heart you are truly leading.

Chapter 21

Open Heart Leadership

It is a risk to open your heart. Most people have had enough heartbreaks and disappointments to make them shut down, become cynical and lose interest in opening up again.

The trouble with shutting down is that failing to open your heart means you become closed off to a whole host of possibilities, including those which could unlock the very solutions you seek.

I once coached a team that was responsible for delivering a programme involving massive change. The previous team had failed – the unofficial reason being a lack of transparency in their ways, which had led to a breakdown in the delivery process.

In actuality, their leader ruled with fear, which had resulted in no one being prepared to be courageous and challenge the status quo. The new leader was deliberately brought in for her different approach. Known for her high emotional intelligence skills, Sarah made it a number one priority to restore trust – thereby building team morale and ensuring that the resultant openness and honesty could drive the programme forward. This open-hearted approach meant that people felt safe enough to raise critical issues and exhibit the level of transparency needed for the complexity involved in deep change.

There is nothing more impressive than watching someone lead with their heart.

It inspires others to be their best selves, and engages people to put their own hearts into what they do. At the most senior levels in organisations, having a high IQ is usually the point of entry. However, in the absence of an open heart people are left cold, with strategic plans that fail to emotionally connect.

Jack was appointed to lead a department that had developed a reputation for being the second-class citizen of the organisation. Over the years it had failed to receive the same amount of care and attention as other areas – and people who worked there knew it. One of the first steps Jack took to address the situation was to ask me to conduct a 'situational assessment'. This involved interviewing colleagues in order to understand their side of the story. One of the key insights that emerged was the clear lack of fairness in resourcing, as this department always seemed to suffer in comparison with others. Jack was determined to rectify the imbalance. However, he knew that in order for the department to achieve an equal playing field in the company, they'd need to deliver great results.

Jack committed to achieving this outcome in a way that would engage and inspire people.

He created a vision for the department that lifted people's spirits, encouraging a new sense of optimism about the future. He invested large amounts of time in listening to people to show how much he cared. He ensured that they focused on developing their lives outside of work as well as in it.

The result?

Over the course of a year, the department increased its performance, and employee engagement shot through the roof – with the outcome that during forecasting for the following year they easily secured the extra funds needed for their future growth.

As a leader, staying connected to your heart ensures that you will demonstrate the right level of emotional engagement, compassion and vulnerability to create an environment where people want to do their best work.

In order to get more in touch with your heart ask yourself, *What is the key question at the heart of my work?* This powerful question directs you to your core, and challenges why you do what you do.

The question at the heart of my own work is, *What is truth?* I am always curious about what is real in every situation, and when I remember to focus on and listen to my heart, it brings the required perspective which allows me to do my best work.

Using your heart as your guide, you can ask yourself the following questions to gain clarity on a wide range of issues such as:

- Brand clarity – *What is the heart of this business, product, or service?*
- Relationship resolution – *What is the heart of this relationship?*
- Strategic direction – *If I were to follow my heart in this situation, what would I do?*
- Team purpose – *What is the heart of our team?*

On a practical level, providing open heart leadership is a great enabler when you have to make tough decisions. The heart has its own energy, which is different from simply applying 'mental logic' to a situation. It requires your emotions to be involved, encouraging you to *feel* what's going on, as well as thinking it through.

One of the hardest decisions that leaders have to face is managing redundancies during downturns. In these highly sensitive situations, the best way to lead is to combine extreme thoughtfulness with heightened empathy in order to support those employees in coming to terms with the tough news, and allow them to work through the required transition to arrive at a positive outcome.

When you connect with your heart, you are truly leading.

Take a Lead

Take a moment and put your right hand on your heart.

- Listen to your heart.

- What is it telling you?

- What does your heart want to say about your leadership?

- Your work? Your life? Your relationships?

Make sure that you consciously connect with your heart in order to be a heartfelt leader.

Leadership is relationship

Great relationships = great results.

Poor relationships = poor results.

Chapter 22

Building Relationship

Think about it.

You can have a great strategy, brilliant product, state-of-the-art technology and effective systems, but without relationship nothing is possible.

I saw this play out vividly when coaching Mark, the resident genius in a high tech company. Mark held a vision for the future, believing himself to be at least five years ahead of everyone else in terms of clarity as to where the company was headed.

However, the trouble with Mark was that he was unable to build a real relationship with his executive colleagues. When I sat down with him it became quickly apparent as to why. His view of the Executive Committee was dismissive, as they didn't appear to grasp his vision quickly enough. He felt that if they didn't get it, the relationship wasn't worth building. A classic case of someone with all the potential to lead a strategic agenda, yet his inability to develop relationship left him out on a limb. When I conducted a robust feedback process on his effectiveness, the clear message that came back from the Executive was that unless he invested in his 'relationship account' his ideas – and his career – would be short-lived in the organisation.

Think about Sir Richard Branson who, with his flamboyant charm, has an almost uncanny knack for developing enduring relationships.

His entrepreneurial flair and risk-taking ability have been written about chapter and verse, yet less is known about his enviable skill at relationship building. During one of my leadership courses, a participant shared a story. Her son, David, was a close friend of Branson's daughter, Holly, while together at university. One day he came bounding home with the news that Holly had invited him to Necker Island for a holiday. His mother said how nice, but that they couldn't really afford it.

The next day she received a phone call from someone called Richard. 'Richard who?' she asked. 'Richard Branson, Holly's dad. Your son is a dear friend of the family and we'd love him to come with us on holiday, obviously all paid for.' The cynic could say that of course he was able to make that offer with his wealth. I would say, instead of telling his daughter to explain the situation, he made the call himself. Wealth and generosity don't always go together. And in fact, Branson did not actually start out wealthy. A central part of his success was achieved by a combination of having original ideas with the ability to develop very close relationships, whether it was with legendary musician Mike Oldfield, whose success helped to finance the origins of Virgin Records, or with his own loyal leadership team which allowed his Virgin empire to take off.

Ask yourself: *On a scale of 1-10 how well do I prioritise my relationships?*

I would suggest that if you score anything less than an 8 you'll be in trouble. In fact the more senior you are in an organisation, the more important relationships become.

Dan was on the verge of joining the Executive Board of his firm. As part of his nomination process he went through a rigorous assessment, involving an occupational psychologist who collected feedback from his key stakeholders. The main theme highlighted by the data about his future success at this level was relationship linked. The concern was that he wouldn't be able to adapt himself to a wide range of different personalities and preferences to forge the level of engagement needed. This formed the basis of our coaching programme, in which we focused on Dan learning the nuances of astute relationship management in an environment of high egos and complex political dynamics.

Given the importance of relationship, it amazes me how rarely I come across people who have formed a clear relationship plan. One tends to think that 'relationships just happen' – which is true, of course. However if you don't deliberately nurture your relationships – at home, with friends or in the workplace – you run the risk that they might not develop in the direction you would like. I'm not talking about being tactical, manipulating and controlling here, nor about divisive behaviour. Put simply, I believe that we suffer from a lack of education and awareness about the importance of:

1) Recognising key relationships
2) Understanding how to develop them
3) Defining what success looks like

Take Lorraine. A classic example of how a leader can fail to pay attention to the right relationships.

Lorraine had spent hours creating a presentation for her Executive Committee, hoping that they would sign off on a big deal she was negotiating. Ahead of the meeting, she had engaged with those members of the Committee who she was close to seeking their perspective on the matter. However, what she had failed to do was to approach those *other* members she was less comfortable with. As a result, she hadn't taken their views and opinions into consideration. As soon as she started her presentation, Lorraine realised her mistake, and saw that the consequences of not having engaged with everyone meant she was not going to get sign-off. A costly mistake.

The following model, known as the Anatomy of Relationships, is a helpful frame to see the relationship dynamics that all too often play out:

Attraction

Appreciation

Familiarity

Expectation

Disappointment

Grievance

BEING RIGHT

It works like this.

The majority of relationships start with a degree of **attraction**, whether it's welcoming a new team member or engaging with someone who is on your wave-length. This leads to a state of **appreciation**, where opinions are valued and contributions recognised. Over time the relationship becomes habituated as a result of the degree of comfort established, and a feeling of **familiarity** sets in. Once habits are set, **expectation** enters the picture and more often than not someone's needs change or develop and expectations may not be met. This is a sensitive place to be in, because usually relationship expectations are not spelled out and it's very difficult to meet them. Once an expectation has not been met, frustration results, which if not expressed or clarified results in **disappointment.** If you allow disappointment to linger, then **grievance** takes over. Now the relationship is in a dangerous place and may be on the verge of disrepair. **Being 'right'** is the lowest place a relationship can go, and is what tends to happen when parties are convinced their point of view is the only legitimate one.

At this level, people use 'evidence' to validate their opinion and try to justify their sense of righteousness. Some relationships can stay stuck here for months, if not years, if at least one party is not prepared and willing to give up the need to be right.

However it's not all doom and gloom.

Any relationship is recoverable if both parties are willing to 'reset' it through the re-contracting of expectations.

For six months, Julie had been working on a high level project. Given that her boss had an extremely stretched workload, Julie's game plan was to limit their interaction so that he didn't have to spend time concerning himself with her performance.

However, at her half-year appraisal it came as a real surprise when she found him rating her as an underperformer. When she enquired as to the reason, it transpired that he had interpreted her lack of communication as a failure to be on top of the project. Julie was then able to explain that her plan had been to involve him on a need-to-know-basis, and that from her point of view everything was well on track. Because the issue had been highlighted, they were now able to 're-contract' their working relationship and it was agreed that Julie would send her boss brief weekly updates, followed by in-depth monthly status reports to keep him fully in the loop. If they had worked this out up front and agreed on their mutual expectations, it would have saved several months of miscommunication.

Ask yourself these vital questions:

- *How effective am I at prioritising my relationships?*
- *Do I clearly articulate my expectations so that others know how best to relate with me?*
- *Am I prepared to let go of the need to be right in order to move my relationships back up to a healthy place?*

At the end of the day, unless you can build enduring relationships you will not be able to lead effectively, so why not commit now to investing in your relationships?

Take a Lead

1. Create your own relationship plan.

2. Jot down which relationships are the most important for you to develop in order to be the best leader you can.

3. Clearly identify what success looks like in each relationship.

4. Commit to taking some specific steps that will take your relationships to the next level of trust and connection.

The truth will set you free

Honesty is the biggest little secret in business.

Chapter 23

Openness & Honesty

When my mentor, Graham Alexander, attended a Q&A session at Chicago Business School with Jack Welch, former CEO of GE, the latter was asked a fundamental question:

'Based on your entire business experience what would you say is the most important factor to be a successful leader?'

Without hesitation, Jack's answer was:

'Candour – openness and honesty.' He added: *'Honesty is the biggest little secret in business'.*

There is no doubt about it. It is rare to come across a leader who has the ability to be honest in a skillful way. I often hear top-level leaders talk about the importance of it – but seeing it in action?

Real honesty requires you to understand the mood of others, recognise how best to meet their needs and provide clear communication.

Probably the most powerful exercise I conduct in my leadership programmes to build this skill is to ask people to tell personal stories about their key life experiences: lessons learned and the conclusions they came to which inform their core values. For some leaders, this takes them so far out of their comfort zone that they are literally unsure if they can do it. However, when they overcome their nerves, the profound effect of speaking their truth is extraordinary. Honesty liberates a person to become more authentic. It creates a magnetic bond with others around you. Think about the power of this. Simply spending a few minutes being honest about who you are and what you stand for can create an emotional connection that lasts a lifetime with others.

I recently asked Graham a similar question to the one Jack Welch was asked: *'Based on your wide experience of coaching leaders, what is the most valuable piece of wisdom you've learned about leadership?'*

He answered along the same lines: *'Be open and honest – except when there is a commercially sensitive reason not to be.'* Going on, he qualified it by describing how honesty ranges from business reality through to personal feelings.

'In my experience a lot of leaders aren't as open and honest as they need to be,' he told me. *'They'll give all sorts of reasons as to why they are not, not all of which are valid in my opinion.'*

Graham shared an example of the time he coached a CEO to disclose more of the hard truth than he would normally consider appropriate. It was during a two-day strategic workshop that Graham was facilitating for the CEO and his Executive Committee.

There'd been lot of change going on in the business and people were feeling uncertain about their futures. In particular, there was speculation about what path the CEO would take regarding his own direction. Within the confines of the workshop, Graham encouraged him to share his deepest feelings about the journey he was on.

This had three major effects:

1) The CEO's team saw their leader as a human being, and this humanity opened up a very different type of interaction between them.

2) The CEO reinforced the importance of being honest by setting an example and encouraging others to be equally candid in their views.

3) The honesty created a lot of empathy and support for the CEO. It helped his team realise how hard it had been for him to manage the level of change, and resulted in them stepping up to give him the support he needed to move forwards.

From an organisational point of view, the trouble with sustaining the hard truth is that there is often such a history of smoke and mirrors that leaders can fall into the trap of avoiding the real issue at hand.

On one occasion, at a company conference I was facilitating, the leader was forced to become more personal and honest about the business reality than he had been in the past. The company was going through particularly tough trading conditions, morale was down and people really wanted to know how it was impacting him and consequentially what he had in mind.

In the afternoon we held a Q&A session with the leader, but I sensed restlessness in the room as his evasiveness was strongly felt. During the break I took him aside, handed him a mug of tea, and told him that to ensure the way forward for the company at this point was to become even more honest and personal. I would not let up. For instance, when we went back in, there was one question which I had to direct to him three times in order to get a sufficiently specific answer to satisfy the audience. I could see that they were expecting the usual bland responses, which would only feed their cynicism more. Although the day stretched the leader far beyond his comfort zone, the feedback from the participants surpassed his expectations with a genuine appreciation of his courage and willingness to treat them like cognisant adults.

There are three key steps to take in order to land the hard truth in a skillful way:

1. Intention

Set a conscious intention to be open and honest. Intention inspires outcome, so your willingness to build greater relationship, resolve issues and move faster to solutions through increased honesty is where you need to start.

2. Emotion

Take responsibility for how you feel. If you sense a degree of emotion around the issue you want to communicate (which is often the case) you must take ownership for your feelings so that no blame or accusation comes across in your communication. Either write down how you are feeling so you can look at it with a clear eye, or discuss it with a trusted confidante who can give you feedback on the way you come across.

3. Information

It's essential to be specific about the data you are sharing so that people can receive and process it. If data lacks clarity it becomes very difficult for the recipient to relate to it.

At the end of the day if you have good intent, take ownership of your feelings and are clear about the facts you are putting across, you will find yourself in a stronger position to share the hard truth constructively.

Take a Lead

1. Commit to telling the truth faster in appropriate ways.

2. Focus on a relationship or situation that requires greater honesty.

3. Ask yourself:

• What is my intention?

• How do I feel?

• What information do I want to share?

Once you have clarity about these 3 steps, you can reflect upon what you will do differently going forwards as you commit to increased openness and honesty.

Trust uncertainty

Leadership is the ability to overcome perceived limitations in order to realise your true potential.

Chapter 24

Step Up

Real leadership is an act of courage. Every day there are challenges to overcome, people to inspire and results to deliver.

Every day you need to step out of your comfort zone and be prepared to stretch yourself in order to think differently and do things differently.

For some personality types, stepping up comes naturally. It is in their DNA to take risks, challenge the status quo and be brave in their decision-making and actions. For others, it takes all their energy to summon enough courage to follow their hearts and act accordingly. One of the wisest sentiments I have come across about stepping up is summed up in Susan Jeffers' seminal book, *Feel the Fear and Do It Anyway*. This concept hit a nerve with millions of people. If you expect the fear to go away before you do something, you will be in for a long wait.

Phil is one of the most talented guys I have come across in the business world. Hugely confident and capable in his field, he was being fast-tracked to take on a significant new leadership role in his organisation. What became apparent was that the major obstacle he faced in saying 'yes' to the new role was self-doubt. He was genuinely concerned that he did not have the ability to raise his game as a leader.

The majority of our work together focused on how to overcome inner states like self-doubt and fear in order to enable Phil to step up to the plate. Over time, he came to recognise that every step forward he took was accompanied by an obstacle to overcome, which once achieved helped him become a better leader.

I believe that these obstacles are simply part of the human condition.

Let's take a look at the four most common ones:

Self–doubt

If you have ever doubted your ability to lead, then welcome to the human race. However, self-doubt is often based on erroneous beliefs such as, *I'm not good enough to lead, I can't lead, I haven't got it in me,* or *I don't know how to lead.* It's important to get at the root of these doubts. For instance, is it that you are not *good enough* to lead, or that you simply need to develop some new leadership skills? Is it true that you *can't* lead, or do you need to have more of a 'can-do' attitude? Do you really not have it *in you* to lead, or do you require the right support to help you lead? Is it a fact that you don't know *how* to lead, or is it an opportunity to seek the right knowledge? By challenging your self-doubt you gain the necessary perspective in order to make the right judgment calls about how best to move forward.

Worry

Worry is addictive. It can even become your job description, 'the worrier'. What often lies behind worry is an attempt to control the future. A futile exercise, because no matter how well you try and plan your life there will be elements that are simply beyond your control. As John Lennon famously said, *'Life is what happens while you are busy making other plans!'* Ask yourself, *'How much worry does it take to solve a problem?'* None. Worry does not solve problems. In fact it creates them. On a physiological level, worry activates the stress hormones cortisol, adrenaline and noradrenaline. As a consequence, perception becomes distorted and you don't think clearly or behave constructively. The initial key to dispelling worry is to take action. Taking action is a way of stepping up and allowing your leadership to become solution oriented.

Cynicism

Cynicism is learnt behaviour that has built up as a result of disappointment. When we hold onto dreams about what we would love to happen and they don't pan out, we become cynical. We've been made promises about how things will be different, only to get more of the same. The trouble with cynicism is that it closes down the creative part of our mind and stops us from seeing the possibilities. When tempted with a cynical response, ask yourself, *How can I see this differently in order to be open to new challenges – and solutions?*

Fear

Franklin D. Roosevelt's famous words, spoken during his First Inaugural Address as the 32nd President of the US were *'The only thing to fear is fear itself.'* Fear does not go away. No matter how experienced, talented or wealthy you are, fear is an essential part of the human experience. Anyone who says 'I have no fear,' frightens the life out of me. It's a form of denial and avoidance. The key to moving through fear is to learn how to befriend it so that it does not frighten you into inaction. As long as you continue to grow, you will experience fear. Every time you move into the unknown, fear accompanies you. Whether it's a new role, a different location, a changing strategy or a fresh approach, fear will be present. But once you move through the fear, it will diminish. Getting used to it means that when you take a new step the fear loosens its grip. One of the distortions that fear brings is the sense that you are alone with it. This is simply not true. It is a global experience. If you are feeling afraid, know that others are too. At the end of the day, having the courage to feel your fear, face it and use it as a source of energy to move forward with greater sensitivity, awareness and presence is a genuine act of leadership.

The difference between good and great leaders are those who are able to step up at will.

Some of the ways that you can consciously do this are to:

1. Raise your self-awareness

Look in the mirror and make an honest assessment as to your strengths and weaknesses. Be brave in the view you have of yourself. Ensure that you are able to accurately describe both your talents and failings in a way that reflects how others see you.

2. Seek feedback

Each time you ask for feedback it is an act of courage as long as you do something with it. One leader I coach describes feedback as a gift and ensures that he receives it on a regular basis to make sure that his version of reality matches that of others.

3. Make appropriate disclosure

When you are prepared to share from your heart it will touch and inspire those around you. This includes the willingness to be vulnerable and reveal your mistakes as well as successes.

4. Take compassionate decisions

Stepping up is about making the tough calls, but you don't have to do it in a ruthless way. Making hard decisions using compassion takes real courage. Anyone can make ruthless decisions and disregard the impact on people – that's easy. Implementing big decisions in a way that shows great empathy and understanding is another matter altogether.

5. Deal with dysfunctional behaviour

Business is easy, people make it hard! Courageous leaders deal directly with toxic behaviours such as aggression, self-promotion, deceit and constant criticism which can wreak havoc with people's lives. They have the means to manage people in a direct way and are prepared to support them in changing their ways.

6. Trust uncertainty

Life is unpredictable. Stepping up means being comfortable with discomfort. It requires us to be prepared to live with the unknown and ride unchartered waters. Trust the inherent process of life itself, knowing that a better outcome will often prevail than one you could have predicted.

Real leadership is the willingness to step up every day.

Take a Lead

1. Which of the four obstacles – self doubt, worry, cynicism or fear – is your biggest challenge?

2. What can you do to remedy this?

3. Ask yourself, *How can I step up today?* in order to turn your courage into action.

Leadership is conversation

'While no single conversation is guaranteed to change the trajectory of a business, a career, a marriage, or a life, any single conversation can.'

Chapter 25

The Power of Conversation

The powerful quote opposite comes from Susan Scott, author of *Fierce Conversations*.

And Alan Webber, co-founder of *Fast Company* magazine recently declared, *'Conversation is the new form of work.'*

Research from *Harvard Business Review* shows that leaders spend around 73% of their time in conversation.

Think about it.

Every meeting, presentation, memo, e-mail, text, tweet, face book entry... it's all a conversation. You could go as far as saying that leadership *is* conversation and that the quality of your conversations reflects the quality of your leadership. If this was the case, how much time and attention do you give to engaging in real value-adding conversations?

Take the following situation. Ron was a highly driven CEO with a passion for winning. Gail possessed one of the best brains in that same organisation – she stood out as an outstanding performer, showing a deep and broad understanding of what was going on. In fact, Ron relied on her heavily to steer the company in the right direction, as well as on her advice regarding the company's general success.

While facilitating one of Ron's leadership meetings, I was surprised to find him directing a lot of his frustration about the team's performance at Gail. When I picked it up with him afterwards, he admitted to being completely unaware of this – however Gail had noticed the strength of his feeling, and I suggested the three of us meet to debrief.

A successful conversation has at its heart a clear intent.

That means the clearer you can be about what you want to happen, the greater the chance that it will.

I started by asking both parties to set out their intent for the conversation.

Ron shared that he wanted to get further clarity as to where Gail was adding value and how she could add even more. Gail wanted to understand if there was anything Ron was not telling her that she needed to know in order to develop their working relationship more successfully.

During the conversation I ensured that both of them put across their point of view clearly, and I kept summarizing what each was hearing to test their real understanding. They could not move on until they felt understood. In fact none of us easily can.

I find it very rare that people take the time to check for understanding and show sufficient empathy. All too often we interrupt, fail to really understand, only show interest in our own agenda or feign interest when we are clearly not that engaged.

I kept holding up the mirror for Ron and Gail until the truth of their situation emerged. Ron realised that he had become over-reliant on Gail and was concerned that if things changed and she moved on, he would be left exposed. Gail shared her concern that Ron's lack of breadth about the business left him open to criticism. She stated her ongoing commitment to helping him succeed, and requested that he be direct in his opinion of her so that she knew exactly where she stood.

This single conversation took them to a different place entirely, and they were able to see how best to work together and resolve any misperceptions that came up along the way. Both agreed that it had saved them several weeks of frustration, and the greater clarity and alignment which resulted meant that they could now play to their strengths.

Having real conversations is one of the biggest time saving devices I know of. It simply sweeps up so many of the misunderstandings that occur in our relationships – whether at work, on the home front or with friends. However there are certain principles that need to be in place to ensure it is possible.

In their enlightening *Harvard Business Review* article, 'Leadership is a Conversation', Boris Groysberg and Michael Slind identify the four I's of successful organisational conversation:

Intimacy
Communication is personal and direct when leaders value trust and authenticity

Interactivity
Leaders talk with their employees, not to them

Inclusion
Leaders relinquish a measure of control over content

Intentionality
Leaders ensure that a clear agenda informs all communication and that strategy emerges from a cross-functional conversation.

I fully agree with these ideas, however the fifth 'I' that I would include is **Inquiry**.

At the heart of a real conversation is the commitment to get into the world of another person, to really inquire about where they are coming from. This means having to suspend your own self-interest, judgments and the need to be 'right'. This desire to be right about your own point of view is probably one of the biggest blockers I encounter to real conversations. It is usually driven by an insecurity and inability to allow others the sufficient space to be listened to. All too often somebody will think they are engaged in a conversation, when in fact they are merely paying lip service and just waiting for the other person to stop talking so that they can make their point. They are simply not that interested in the 'other'.

I once worked on a strategic partnership between a client and customer group. In theory they were reliant on each other for their success, but much of the time they complained about the partnership, had low trust and were adversarial in their approach, which meant that their conversations failed to get past their seemingly conflictual agendas. In order for value-adding conversations to take place, we worked together to find a basic principle to guide them: *Assume good intent. Anything else is a misunderstanding.* From this point onwards, whenever a conversation derailed they learnt to revert back to this principle, reminding them of their true commitment and intent.

The more you work the muscles of empathy and intent, the more you will develop the capability for value-adding conversations.

Take a Lead

Before any big conversations you have, conduct a conversation health check, asking yourself:

- How trusting and authentic am I being in this relationship?

- How willing am I for this conversation to be a genuine collaboration?

- How open am I to seeing things differently?

- How clear am I about the purpose and agenda for the conversation?

- How well do I empathise and seek a win/win outcome?

Let your conversations be the catalyst for inspiration.

Your profession as a leader is to listen

Generous listening is one of the best investments

a leader can make.

Chapter 26

The Common Cold of Leadership

In one of his video clips from *The Little BIG Things*, Tom Peters, provocative management guru, asks the following question, based on New York Times bestselling title, *How Doctors Think*.

He challenges the viewer to guess how long it takes, on average, before a doctor will interrupt a patient while listening to their symptoms being described. Given, of course, that this is the doctor's prime source of information in understanding the patient's condition.

Any ideas?

18 seconds.

When I play this clip during my leadership programmes, there is unanimous agreement within the groups as to the truth this reveals about them. Most leaders find that they are 18-second leaders!

Nodding heads. Pretending. Waiting to reply. These are mild symptoms of the common cold of leadership.

Ignoring. Interrupting. Shutting down. These are the more extreme symptoms.

What I'm referring to is the failure to listen.

Poor listening is one of the biggest mistakes a leader can make. I see it in every meeting. I experience it in most conversations. No matter how good you think you are at listening, I will pretty much guarantee that you are exercising about 50% of your listening capacity.

My own research shows two schools of thought:

1: *The quality of content determines the quality of listening*. In other words, interesting content and delivery inspire attentive listening.

2: *The quality of the listener determines the quality of delivery*. Whereby the listener's attentiveness inspires the speaker or presenter to perform at their best.

I have a distinct memory of this dynamic from my days as a violinist. On many occasions, having practiced a piece of music close to perfection, when it came to performing, I found that if the audience acted as if they'd rather be somewhere else – whispering, rustling of shoes, coughing, children chattering – my performance would be hijacked and I couldn't play at my best. However, if I played in front of an audience who hung onto my every note, who listened with generosity, then my performance could excel.

Remember in Chapter 14, how Bill Clinton was the most admired leader referenced on leadership programmes? It was because of his remarkable listening ability. Each of the several people who had had the privilege of meeting him described the same powerful experience of his generous listening. A powerful example cited was how during a 3-day leadership summit with over 2,000 delegates, a question was asked on the first day by one of the delegates. It didn't get answered. But on Day 3, Clinton went back and referenced that particular question – using no notes – acknowledging that the question had been bypassed.

A person who listens intently, paying 100% attention, can leave a lifetime's impact.

And how about this? A snippet recounted about former basketball champion, Magic Johnson recounted by Steve, a Sales Manager at a hotel resort in Hawaii where Magic used to stay during the summer when resting up from his demanding schedule.

It was mid-August and Magic's birthday, so Steve brought a birthday cake, in the shape of a basketball, and bottle of Bollinger down to Magic's favourite sun lounger by the pool. They chatted, and afterwards Steve thought nothing more of it. The following summer Magic returned to the resort. Steve still worked there and once again, on Magic's birthday, he brought down another cake and bottle of vintage Bollinger. They began to talk and Steve was blown away when Magic asked him how he was getting along with his family and whether he had purchased the apartment on the hill which he'd told him about the year before. Now, in the last 365 days Magic had experienced a relatively busy year playing in the Olympics as well as enjoying another winning season with the LA Lakers. No doubt he had been involved in thousands of conversations with a wide variety of people; however he had listened sufficiently closely to Steve to be able to recall their conversation. This left a marked impression on the sales manager, which he carries to this day.

How do you want to be remembered as a leader? As someone who was absent, ignoring others, or as someone with a genuine interest and care in others and able, as a consequence, to exercise authentic listening.

We all have a natural ability to be great listeners, however it takes a genuine desire to apply our listening capacity. However, before embarking on the journey of changing the way you listen, ask yourself if you're really up for it as there's nothing more disconcerting than a leader who has been on a 'listening course' and comes back to work full of such good intention that he or she starts unnerving people – by mirroring their body language, repeating back what they've said, and desperately trying to ignore the vibrating phone in their top pocket! It even gets taken home when leaders recount how they start listening to their partner only to find them suspiciously wondering if they're having an affair, crashed the car or overspent on the credit card!

The key to listening is being authentic.

If you find yourself genuinely distracted, my suggestion is to let others know that you're unable to be fully present so as to better manage their expectation. For instance, if someone approaches you to engage in a meaningful conversation and you've got something on your mind, find out how urgent the conversation is and whether it can wait until you are able to give it the attention it deserves.

Sounds so simple, doesn't it?

Yet few of us do it. My experience shows that people would far rather wait until a leader has the capacity to listen to them and truly engage in a conversation, than attempt one only to find them distracted or frequently glancing at their in-box. If I'd put a pound in my pocket every time I heard of an employee attending a one-on-one meeting with their manager only to find themselves being treated as secondary to the manager's pressing e-mails; or presenting at a meeting while others are intent on their iPads, I'd be a very rich man.

When you listen, bring generous ears. In working environments, most people have critical ears and are constantly looking for rights and wrongs, applying judgment, analysing and imposing their own agenda on others. Although these can be helpful traits they need to be blended with the commitment to be wholehearted in our listening, which is an ability that can be honed. Empathy is most clearly demonstrated through listening, creating deep connections between people. By listening well, you will emotionally connect with others, deepen your understanding, and in showing how much you care become able to enjoy the rewards of improved relationships.

Take a Lead

- Commit to generous listening.

- Be aware of the distractions that limit your ability to listen.

- Ask yourself, *What stops me from listening?*

- Be aware of your key interferences and manage them accordingly, so that you can become an effective listener.

A leader is a storyteller

A story is a way of perceiving reality through a different lens.

Chapter 27

The Magic of Story

Graham led the Asia-Australasia region in his organisation.

A hugely respected figure, I had the privilege of watching him in action during the small, intimate evenings which he set up for groups of his senior leaders attending the company's Leadership Development programme. The purpose of these particular sessions was to give the participants a rich insight into Graham's leadership story.

Graham introduced the first evening by inviting the participants to ask him any question they wanted. No topic was off limits. One memorable evening, a senior leader asked him: What do you actually *do* as a leader?

Graham's response was simple and poignant.

'I don't *do* anything,' he said. 'I am a storyteller. I spend my time with investors, customers and the media sharing stories about how great you all are.' Graham was very clear that the biggest contribution he could make to the company was to inspire and engage others through 'telling stories'.

Storytelling is an art, which some people can do naturally and others need to spend more time developing. It starts with the understanding that the most powerful way to engage others is through a compelling story. I find that one of the most important keys to becoming a great storyteller is a willingness to speak from your heart. Combine that with your imagination and you have a powerful, genuine tool in your hands. This way exists in sharp contrast with those in senior leadership positions who speak from their heads, failing to connect with others as a result of their corporate blandness or lack of imagination, who show little or no sensitivity to the experience of being on the receiving end of their communications.

I was troubled on one occasion by working with a leader who had a series of important presentations to give his people on a road show they were doing around the UK. Unfortunately, despite my interventions, he overloaded his people with so much information that no one could fully absorb it. Clearly, he was trying to mask his own insecurities, and staying in his own comfort zone by focusing on the minutiae of detail, refusing to open his heart and share his real thoughts and feelings about the business or his own leadership role. The penny finally dropped when he read feedback from some of his employees, which said in no uncertain times, *'Death by PowerPoint is a crime to humanity!'* and *'Is there actually a human being behind these slides?'*

I contrast this is to the effect that leaders have who are prepared to open their hearts and let people into their world.

Christine walked into a high-pressured operational environment where the previous leader had been known for having a very low engagement level with his team.

One of her first acts was to set up an offsite get-together for her leadership team, far away from the demands of work. She was determined to take a lead and set the tone with the team in the way that she intended it to continue – open, transparent and direct. Christine told them her 'story' based on the good, bad and the ugly of her leadership journey so far. She spoke from the heart about what she stood for, her vision for the team, the qualities she brought to the department, the areas she needed to improve in, and how they could get the best out of her. Christine's only slides were photographs to illustrate her points. The team was gripped. Her thirty-minute story led to a dialogue lasting two hours, prompted by the team who couldn't get enough.

Storytelling is not for the chosen few.

Everyone is born with the potential to be a convincing storyteller. We see it in children; each one is able to make a story from their world: I remember when my youngest son, at two, conjured up magical stories about the snails and worms he was playing with, and I sat there transfixed. Children are not limited by the conditioning that we receive in our education that somehow unfortunately colours our innate ability to tell stories. I remember getting the message at school that nothing to do with English was up my alley, and I certainly developed the impression that I was no good at storytelling. What I realised later was that I simply had to find my story, and my own way of telling it. Now I do it through writing and presentations. I make things personal, I trust my voice, I have fun, and I look to both inform and entertain.

One communications expert who coaches leaders on this subject encourages 'pub talk'. She gets leaders to imagine that they are down at their local pub tasked with the challenge of having to engage everyone over and above the noise of the drinking and talking by delivering their message in a simple and entertaining way.

One of my closest friends, Andy Thrasyvoulou, is the visionary behind the well-known hospitality brand, myhotel. Andy uses the word 'edutainment' to describe the essence of a great story: in other words the ability to combine education with entertainment. He uses this approach in the induction programmes for his hotel group.

Based in London, over 50% of myhotel's employees speak English as a second language. So in order to help them to engage with each other, Andy has everyone tell a meaningful story from their homeland. They do this in their mother tongue, and with the assistance of people in the group, it gets translated into English. As people tell their stories, connections are made and a bond is formed, which exactly resonates with the bond Andy wants his team to make with their guests.

As you learn to become a compelling storyteller, it's vital to listen to your heart, trust your inner voice and be authentic. There is nothing more powerful than someone who is prepared to engage others from the depths of their being. It transcends both cultural and language differences. It goes beyond different opinions; and it opens doors for looking at things in new ways, enabling genuine alignment and connection.

Take a Lead

- When last did you visit TED.com?

- You'll be amazed at the fantastic variety of people telling their story in 15 minutes or less.

- Commit to doing your own TED docu-story.

- What would you choose to reveal/say/explore about your world and how would you translate it into a great story?

- Film yourself doing one.

- Commit to speaking from your head and heart in all future interactions to combine information and entertainment.

Great thoughts lead to great results

How much time do you spend actually thinking?

Chapter 28

Think Time

As Nancy Kline, renowned expert on thinking environments and best-selling author of *Time to Think* puts it: *'The quality of everything we do depends on the quality of the thinking we do first.'*

In fact, there is direct relationship between the quality of our thinking and the quality of our results. However, one of the biggest challenges in today's workplace is that most leaders are usually too busy to think. Do you, for instance, manage to schedule yourself 'think time' on a regular basis in order to increase the quality of your leadership?

Consider the difference you could make by consciously committing to improving your quality of thinking. According to the National Science Foundation, we think around 50,000 thoughts a day. What if we were to decide to make just 1% (500 thoughts) of real value?

A good place to start is by identifying when and where you do your best thinking.

When I ask leaders this question, take a guess what comes up. The boardroom? The office? In front of my laptop?

Not at all.

The answer is more along the lines of: on a course (golf not educational), travelling (in the car, on a train or plane), taking a shower, walking the dog or while on holiday…

I challenge every employer to encourage their employees to play more golf, have longer showers and take more holidays, as there is no doubt that they would benefit greatly from the increased quality-time thinking. As of yet, I don't think this has been acted upon. So in the meantime, let's work out how to harness it better.

One of the great thinkers of our time is Bill Gates. Someone who worked closely with him during Microsoft's early days describes a 'Bill Gates moment' as being Gates reclining with his feet up on his desk, hands behind his head apparently doing nothing at all. However, what he was doing very actively was thinking. This sent an important message to people at Microsoft – that thinking matters. The company even issued everyone with red 'thinking caps' so that people could sit at their desks and when they needed time for genuine thinking, they knew that when they put the caps on they wouldn't be disturbed.

Another innovative thinker was, of course, Steve Jobs. In Walter Isaacson's exclusive biography he reveals that one of Jobs' great strengths was his ability to focus his thinking. As Jobs put it, 'Deciding what not to do is as important as deciding what to do.'

In order to make thinking a real priority you need to challenge how you regard it. For instance, if your definition of work does not include thinking, then you won't see the importance of it and will fail to give it any time. On the other hand, if your definition of work does include thinking then you will find it easier to make the time for thinking activities like vision, prioritising and planning.

I believe that in our highly task-focused environments we have forgotten the art of thinking.

Psychologist and Nobel Peace Prize winner in Economics, Daniel Kahneman, challenges us to deepen our understanding of thinking in his latest book Thinking, Fast and Slow. It is a fascinating account of our two modes of thought: System 1, which is fast, instinctive and emotional and System 2, which is slower, more deliberate and logical. One of the central points Kahneman makes is that in our speeded up lives we tend to place too much reliance on System 1 and that we need to balance it out with System 2, in order to integrate our human judgment with the deeper reflection that happens through real thinking.

Below are four key reasons why we fail to give thinking sufficient time and attention:

1. Fear of thinking

As one client said: 'What if I set out to think about an initiative only to find out I have no thoughts on the matter?' Or as another shared, 'My fear of thinking is that I won't like what I think.' A useful way to overcome the fear of thinking is to adopt the practice of one of the best thinkers I know. He has a discipline whereby he schedules a 'think day' on a monthly basis, carving out this precious time and making a list of topics he will think about at the appointed time.

2. Resistance to thinking

A very common trait that I am only too familiar with is what happens when you *have* made the effort to schedule valuable think time. Suddenly everything else becomes that much more pressing! If you've planned 'think time' at home, then clearing your desk, going through your old files, even doing the washing up suddenly becomes of great interest.

And if you're at the office, it's amazing how many tasks you can find which take you away from your original purpose within minutes. All resistance is an excuse. We use it as a distraction to letting thinking happen. The only way to overcome resistance is discipline. For example, when I write, I set myself time and word count targets to ensure that I override any resistance. My usual commitment is to set aside two hours to write 1000 words. Although the initial quality of thinking might not be that high, I would much rather come back and do a rewrite than succumb to the tyranny of resistance.

3. Too guilty to make the time

In most work environments success is measured by the *amount of task completed* vs. the *quality of thinking invested.* When this is the case it often leads to people feeling guilty if they prioritise time to think. One leader I coached did his best thinking in the gym, before getting to work. Often, when the body is on autopilot the mind is able to roam freely, naturally finding the subjects that most require attention. Having the time and space to exercise helped give Henry the mental clarity required to resolve many of the issues on his mind. However he usually felt too guilty to do it, as it felt like taking time off. The guilt ran so deep, that even when his very supportive line manager demanded that he go to the gym, he struggled to do it. Giving people permission to think is a pre-requisite for developing quality thinking environments, and then following it up by the act of giving recognition for thinking. One enlightened leader encouraged his people to replace the hours spent on creating glossy power point presentations with simple one page hand written thought documents as a way of promoting his passion for thinking.

4. Exhaustion

It's hard to think when we're exhausted. However, given the demands of travel schedules, back-to-back meetings and overflowing inboxes, it's only too easy to end up totally knackered – not a great recipe for quality thinking. As a leader it's essential to manage your energy in order to enable your best thinking. For instance, one leader I coach does her best thinking in the morning. So we work together to ensure that she prioritises her schedule around her energy, putting in her think time for big projects and challenging meetings in the first part of the day when she's fresh. This is in contrast to one manager whose team deliberately avoids him on Friday afternoons, as this is when he is at his lowest ebb and his thinking far from clear.

Learn to make thinking a priority.

Thinking is not something you bolt onto your 'day job'. It is intrinsic to your day job! Engaging in quality thinking is one of the major contributions that you will make, not only to your work, but to your whole life as well. Your ability to think with more attention and increased focus will make an immeasurable difference to how effective you are, how insightful, how open, clear and inspiring.

Take a Lead

Build up your thinking muscle by scheduling five minutes of quality 'think time' a day.

Ring fence this time so that nothing can disturb it. You could select a topic in advance to think about, or see what emerges in the moment and dependent on your thinking style you might want to write your thoughts down, create a mind map, speak them out loud, or simply silently think.

Leaders Dream

Can you open your mind, entertain new ideas, see things differently, generate options and even think the unthinkable?

Chapter 29

Think Possibility

We all know about positive thinking. Now, while I am a believer in positivity, I sometimes find a certain naivety – and even something vaguely annoying – at play amongst positive thinkers.

Too many times have I come across strong advocates of the method who almost terrorise others, using what can only be called subtle scare tactics to convince them to try and think positively. *If you think negative thoughts they will manifest*, is the all-too popular phrase, causing people to feel anxious about their concerns and worrying that their negative thoughts will materialise – which results in thinking positively from a fearful place. This is not positive thinking, nor is it helpful. There is a particular technique called 'reframing', which when done well has good results. It encourages people to turn situations around by looking at what is positive about them. For instance, if someone has been made redundant they should try to see it as an opportunity for a new beginning. Or, if a boss gives you unjust negative feedback, it is a chance to build your inner resilience.

Although reframing has good intent behind it, it's essential that it be applied with care, sensitivity and empathy alongside emotional honesty in order for a situation to be really understood.

In an organisational context, the tyranny of positive thinking often shows up in marketing departments, where it's made out that every new idea or product being promoted is the next best thing. The trouble is that this is often not the case and when the idea or product is exposed for what it really is, the department risks yet another a knock in credibility.

The difference with 'thinking *possibility*' is that it does not deny or avoid your current reality in trying to get you to believe something that is not true.

However, it does challenge you to be creative in your thinking, move out of your comfort zone and stretch yourself to see things differently. In truth, all great acts of creation start with planting a seed of possibility.

Simon Woodroffe, founder of Yo! Sushi and one of the first entrepreneurs on the BBC show 'Dragons Den' is one of the most original and inspiring possibility thinkers I know. We met through a mutual friend in the early 90's when Simon was working in the media. Frustrated by the limitations of his job, he went on a trip to Japan and discovered 'conveyor belt' sushi. When he got back home, he got the crazy idea to open the very first such sushi bar in the UK, delivering the food at 8 cm per second to the customer – complete with waitresses in PVC. The PVC never materialised, but he succeeded in overcoming a series of obstacles, and opening the doors to what has become the most famous of sushi brands – practically a household name – in the UK. Simon continues to 'think possibility' through the creation of Yo! Hotel and his latest idea, Yo! Home.

When I spoke to Simon about tips for possibility thinking he told me three things that encouraged him along the way:

1) *Nurture your creativity.* Simon claims that he was lucky to leave school with only a couple of good grades, but his creativity intact. He believes that we all have inherent creativity, but our education and society tend to knock it out of us. It's essential to nurture creativity like a newborn child.

2) *Carry a notebook.* Become an ideas junkie. Simon writes down all his ideas, no matter how seemingly insignificant. He believes that this way you never miss an opportunity to note a possibility.

3) *The 90-day rule.* Give an idea 90 days before dismissing it. We tend to dismiss our thinking too quickly. Once you have an idea worth exploring, give it time to germinate before deciding what you want to do with it.

One of the often unforeseen problems occurring in organisations is that while people get employed for their innovative sense of possibility, they often quickly get institutionalised into the current system of thinking that exists in the culture.

Brian was a brilliant 'possibility thinker' and came in to head up the Sales and Marketing Division of a FTSE 100 company. Initially his leaders sought his ideas. He was invited into the Executive Committee's meetings on a regular basis and received encouraging recognition for his thinking. However, after a few months the enthusiasm began to dry up – and so did Brian's thinking. When I reached him he was disillusioned and ready to quit. Demoralised by what appeared to be the lack of buy-in to his thinking, he couldn't work it out.

How could there be such an apparent turn in the tide after such a bright and promising start? When I interviewed the Executive Committee to get feedback on the situation the message came back loud and clear. Although people really appreciated Brian's energy, thinking and creativity they didn't believe the organisation was ready to take on board such radical concepts. Following the assimilation of this insight he was able to go back and re-engage with the Executive, with a greater sense of empathy about how to socialise new thinking in a risk-averse environment.

The trouble is that if organisations don't allow room for thinking possibility where will the new ideas come from?

Equally, if you don't create space for possibility in your own life what price will you pay? My wife, Veronica, has a natural ability for possibility thinking, which challenges my limits. For instance, when we started a family I was content with having one child, after the birth of our amazing daughter. However, my wife comes from a family of eight, so after the birth of our second child I hadn't considered the possibility of bringing a third child into the world. Well, we did, and he has completed our family.

On the home front, Veronica is an interior designer. Up until that point my thinking about a house was that functional was good, and IKEA economical. However, she entertains very different thinking and as a result we live in a beautiful environment filled with an eclectic mix of antiques and modern finds. It's what changed our house into a home.

I love playing with the question, *'What if?'* to open up to new possibilities.

Ask yourself questions like, *What if I was 10% less busy and yet more productive? What if I had an answer to every problem? What if I genuinely trusted the brilliance of others? What if my relationships got better and better? What if I lived my life on purpose? What if I were able to adapt my leadership style intuitively to every situation?*

How would you feel considering these possibilities?

The steps to becoming a possibility thinker involve:

1) *Giving yourself time and space.* As we have noted it's hard to think when you have no time. It's even harder to think possibility when you're under a huge amount of pressure.

2) *Suspending judgment.* It's only too easy for our analytical skills to kick in and trash our thinking.

3) *Seeking out possibility thinkers.* Spend time with others who stimulate your own thinking.

4) *Engaging in activities that stretch your thinking.* What are you reading? What are you watching? Where do you spend your time?

If you live on autopilot, break it up in order to allow yourself to consider a whole host of new possibilities.

Take a Lead

Ask yourself:

How can I entertain more real possibility in my

- Work

- Life

- Relationships

Delight, gladness, pleasurable emotion due to well-being or satisfaction, exultation of spirit

Joy is your birthright. It is not something you have to earn, deserve or pay for.

Chapter 30

Follow your Joy

What is your joy? One way of looking at leadership is having the knowledge of what joy means to you and finding the courage to follow it.

In my experience of business, I have observed that when leaders follow their joy they are at their most creative and able to add the most value. When they are out of touch with it they become transactional or to-do oriented in their approach, and their potential is diminished.

Western society tends to put the work principle and joy at two opposite ends of the spectrum. It is a mystery why, as when we follow our joy we play to our strengths, and are more productive. Unfortunately, it is rare to come across leaders who follow their joy. As one leader reflected when I encouraged him to start exploring the concept: *'How can I free myself from the chains of corporate slavery that bind me, because if I follow my joy I'm out?'*

Yet the challenge of following your joy is not limited to the corporate world. For instance, although I have always been self-employed, I have struggled to be guided by joy.

Growing up in a highly specialised music environment, I found that what constantly drove me was the puritanical work ethic – discipline and the pursuit of perfection. And though these traits are useful up to a point, they do not nurture the seeds of joy. In fact, I taught myself to override my true joy and became an expert at following other people's instructions. It took a great deal of soul searching to understand that my own joy lay in helping people. I discovered that there was nothing I loved more than enabling others to put the jigsaw pieces of their lives together to make a better fit.

As I write this chapter today, I look around and see that I have come a long way in the pursuit of joy. I am sitting in the Tuscan countryside, staying at the beautiful home of some close friends. I have just returned from my morning jog accompanied by the village church bells. The kids are eating freshly picked figs for breakfast. Our plan for the day is to relax at the local lake followed by a medieval festival up in the hills. And I have carved out some time to write. It is a pleasure and delight to sit down and allow the creative juices to flow.

This is the gift of following your joy.

I can hear the cynic in you saying, *This is all very well but what does following your joy look like?*

In truth, anything.

For one client, the MD of a train operating company, it is delivering a brilliant passenger experience for the customers he serves. For another, a Sales Director, joy includes the creative element of putting a brush to canvas and painting landscapes alongside his love of closing deals. For a CEO father it is spending time with his kids regardless of what form the activity takes. His joy comes from watching his children learn and grow.

Joy lies in the essence of what you are focused on. It is what brings meaning to your life. What feels right. It doesn't require you to change your job, marriage, or where you live.

In fact when I'm coaching people on finding and following their joy, one of the first agreements we make is to not rush into any reactive decision that may change anything in their existing circumstances.

So, at the end of the day, how do you follow your joy? Below are ten important pointers to guide you in the right direction:

Focused attention

You are completely absorbed in the moment. Nothing can distract you. It is all-consuming and there is nowhere else you would like to be.

Relaxed concentration

You feel a great sense of relaxation whilst being 100% concentrated on what's in hand. You have a heightened awareness of what's around you, however nothing distracts you.

Increased energy

You are truly energised by what you are engaged with. For instance, when you are around people who are a joy to be with you are energised and when you are focused on a project that is a joy your energy increases.

Sense of possibility

Your imagination is wide open. You see things with fresh eyes. You believe that solutions are at hand, even if faced with great adversity and challenge.

Heightened will

You tap into your deepest determination to overcome any obstacles, and find within yourself an unrelenting commitment to achieving your desires.

Support from others

You discover that people are at and on your side. They are inspired by your joy and want to support it, often in ways that you didn't anticipate or imagine.

Timeless state

The clock stops. You are not governed by time. You have a very direct experience of being in the present, the here and now.

Intrinsic reward

The reward is joy itself. You would do your work whether you were being paid or not (although those who follow their joy tend to receive better remuneration). You become more altruistic in your outlook and selfless in your approach.

Brings out the best in you and others

You flourish in your relationships. You excel in your performance. You access new dimensions of creativity. You go beyond what you think is possible.

Joy is infectious

People want to know what you're on! They can feel the magic and want to share it. Ultimately it helps others discover their joy.

Joy is your birthright. It is not something you have to earn, deserve or pay for. However, to follow your joy you must be prepared to relinquish the concept of 'no pain, no gain'. You must be willing to let go of the guilt and judgment that can hold you back from getting in touch with joy.

Following your joy is first and foremost an inner commitment to living your life on purpose.

Take a Lead

Ask yourself:

• *What am I most passionate about?*

• *What do I love?*

• *What is my joy?*

Before making any changes to your circumstances, be prepared to commit to follow your joy each day and observe the impact on your energy, focus and inspiration.

How much do you believe in the value of enjoyment?

Evidence shows that when people enjoy what they do they do a great job.

Chapter 31

Enjoying Work

Do you work in an environment that has been deliberately set up for you to enjoy your job? It never ceases to amaze me how often this essential factor gets overlooked.

Over the years I have even encountered active hostility to the idea of work as an enjoyable concept. However, I believe that 'leaders' who ignore their employees' enjoyment levels are outdated and will eventually see the negative impact on both employee engagement and ultimately results. Today's leader recognises the importance of ensuring that people enjoy what they do and actively provides models for what this looks like.

Alan is one of those leaders I'm referring to. He firmly believes that if your vision consists of matching the right talent with the right opportunities, establishing clear targets and expectations and then letting people get on with enjoying the job at hand, then great results will be the natural consequence.

I coached him as he transitioned into heading up a large department consisting of several thousand people. He had inherited a team that was pretty demoralised: their history one of having been 'beaten up' by their main investor who'd sucked them dry with impossible demands.

Alan scheduled an offsite event to start the journey of creating a vision for the future. He opened it by sharing his aspirations for developing an environment in which people could be authentic, find real meaning in what they do, learn and develop their skill-sets and enjoy their work. His main commitment was a promise to help remove any interference in order to make this possible. Naturally, the initial response was one of cynicism and disbelief. The team had become so accustomed to the whip that this picture was almost a stretch too far. However, when he laid out the alternatives – keep the status quo or quit – they were willing to get on board and give it a try.

The process of shifting the culture did not happen overnight. Culture change never does. So we did it in stages. Once the senior team was on board, they then focused on going out and engaging their people. A series of road shows were set up to share the new vision, accompanied by large doses of listening through focus groups and one-to-one conversations. People were asked to identify what they already enjoyed about their work and to share ideas of how their enjoyment could be increased. Suggestions came thick and fast, such as sharing success stories in order to recognise and celebrate best practice; cross-functional role shadowing so that people could learn what others do; social events to get to know each other; and lunch-and-learn sessions for ongoing personal and professional development. Some of these ideas got implemented, others didn't. However, everyone appreciated the serious commitment to making work enjoyable.

It does seem remarkable that leaders need to give permission for people to enjoy their work. However, conditioned fear and guilt are usually the blocks we need to overcome along the way.

Does this scenario sound familiar?

It's the annual end-of-year conference and the CEO stands up to acknowledge the achievements of the year. For a few minutes everyone feels good, however it is short-lived as out comes the dreaded word, 'But…'

Suddenly all the life is zapped from the room. The CEO continues with, 'Next year is going to be our most difficult year yet. We have got even more stretching targets in the most unpredictable trading conditions ever witnessed.'

Any concept of enjoyment has firmly been squashed and people are back to a survivalist mode. While certainly not advocating an ostrich approach to dealing with the very real challenges that leaders face today, or suggesting false positivity, I am simply talking about the need for a genuine recognition of the fact that *when people enjoy what they do, they do a better job.*

I believe the main block to enjoyment at work has its roots in a puritanical work ethic, founded on concepts such as *No pain, no gain* or *Success is 99% perspiration, 1% inspiration* or *To get ahead takes effort plus more effort.*

Other more personal beliefs I've encountered include:

- If it gets too good I'll have further to fall, therefore I'd better not let myself enjoy my work too much.
- Other people will get envious if I enjoy my work and will try to sabotage it.
- I'll get overly obsessed if I enjoy my work, to such a degree that I could neglect other areas like friends and family.
- I won't be taken seriously if I appear to be enjoying my work.
- I won't deliver the required results if I'm busy enjoying myself.

And then there's the guilt. *If I'm enjoying myself I'm slacking. I don't have a right to enjoy my work. I can't be paid well and enjoy what I do. If I'm enjoying my work but others aren't, I won't be perceived as a team player.*

These beliefs mean that the idea of enjoyment being a competitive advantage stays a foreign concept, but we must go beyond this limiting reality.

The 2012 London Olympics was a brilliant example of enjoyment in action, while delivering world-class results. Watching the events was a breathtaking experience as one observed the ability to combine talent, opportunity and clear goals with unbelievable discipline. The level of enjoyment that accompanied great performances was clearly tangible. The images of Usain Bolt, as he proved himself yet again the world's fastest runner, will remain for a lifetime. Peak performance, enjoyment. They go together. And not only in the field of sport.

Musicians across the world genuinely enjoy the opportunity to create a unique performance each time they play. I'd go so far as to say that you can't produce a really memorable perfomance as a musician unless you are enjoying yourself; it opens the path to brilliance, and the audience will always pick up on it. I recently saw a performance of Sting, with an amazing array of talented musicians, and they were clearly having a ball. I also saw the Rolling Stones live and watching a near-70 Mick Jagger singing his heart out was pure inspiration.

I would go as far as saying that greatness in any profession is by necessity marked by a sign of true enjoyment.

What do you enjoy about your work?

I have posed this question to countless leaders over the years and it tends to be met with a cautious response.

Why is that?

Sometimes they don't want to admit what they enjoy.

Sometimes they genuinely don't know.

The trouble is that if you truly don't know what you enjoy in your work it will limit the effectiveness of your leadership. Engaging and inspiring others when you are not enjoying yourself is very tough. If not impossible. I once worked in an organisation where the leader demonstrated zero enjoyment. He also had certain habits that impacted the enjoyment of others. For instance, each week he wrote a blog that was e-mailed around the office on a Friday afternoon. In theory, it is a great concept to hear from your CEO about the events of the week and what is on his mind. However, no matter how many successes were clocked up he would unfailingly dedicate his final paragraph to some element of doom and gloom, ensuring that nobody could remotely look forward to their forthcoming weekend.

I will ask you again, *What do you enjoy about your work?*

But be specific. For example, don't just say people. What is it about people that you really enjoy? If it's about a sense of achievement, what is it exactly that you enjoy achieving?

On a personal note these are some of the ingredients that make my work truly enjoyable:

- Helping people grow and go beyond what others expect of them
- Partnering up with successful clients and supporting them in increasing their success
- Sharing ideas that make a difference in people's lives
- Challenging people to face their fears and break through to new levels of clarity and freedom
- Gaining instant feedback as a result of working directly with people
- Learning and growing as a result of every piece of work I do

Believe me, this wasn't always the case.

It has been an ongoing journey – and sometimes a struggle – over the last twenty-five years to arrive at a place where I can honestly say that I enjoy what I do and feel blessed to be where I am.

One of my biggest wishes for you to is to experience enjoyment every day in your chosen work, life and relationships.

Take a Lead

Ask yourself honestly: *What do I enjoy about my work?*

Make a list of the top 5 reasons why you enjoy what you do:

1. _____

2. _____

3. _____

4. _____

5. _____

and ensure that you allow yourself to experience at least 80% enjoyment levels on a consistent basis.

Confidence builds capability

What does it take to be your best self?

Chapter 32

The Confidence Factor

Do any of these phrases sound familiar?

Just wait until they find out who I really am, then they'll get rid of me.

I've kidded them for years about my ability, but I don't think I'll be able to get away with it for much longer.

No matter what I do, it simply is not good enough.

That's the voice of self-doubt.

Believe me when I say that every great leader I have encountered either suffers from, or has suffered from, a lack of confidence at some point. It's simply part of being human.

In fact, I would go as far as saying that anyone who denies experiencing self-doubt is seriously out of touch with reality. Or they're being dishonest. However, self-doubt is not the real issue when it comes to confidence. What makes the difference is *how* you relate to self-doubt; this is what determines whether you learn and grow from the experience, or shrink and wither.

Harry had finished the year on a high. He had recently won numerous awards for his innovative marketing campaigns for one of the most well known brands in the UK, and enjoyed a fun Christmas with his family. He was happily gearing up for another successful year ahead. On the Friday just before New Year's, he received a call from his manager to attend an urgent meeting. Sitting in his boss's office a few hours later, he could barely take in the news. That despite his success, the company had had to make cuts and was making his position redundant. Harry could either take the redundancy package, or wait to see if another position became available. In shock, and with his confidence shattered, he accepted the offer of redundancy and retreated home to lick his wounds.

But it didn't end there.

A few weeks later, Harry received another call from his ex-manager requesting a second meeting. The news on this occasion? That the company had done an about-turn and wanted to offer Harry his job back. The manager admitted that they had made a mistake: they'd taken Harry's success for granted and now, faced with the prospect of not having him leading the brand, realised what an integral member of the company he was. Would he consider coming back?

Harry and I caught up over a strong coffee to discuss his options and what this scenario had uncovered. He was understandably and justifiably angry by the way he had been treated, and tempted to throw his toys out of the pram and walk away. However, when we dug deeper into what had happened, it transpired that the whole experience had triggered his biggest fear. Redundancy. The sense of rejection and perceived negation of his talent had brought him to his knees and made him seriously question his ability. Through our coaching conversations Harry came to recognise that he could either go down a path of self-doubt, or he could stay with the facts of the company's management mistakes, and use this opportunity to increase his self-confidence.

Let's take it apart.

Harry, when challenged to look at his situation, saw that he had become overly dependent on external factors, such as the approval of his company and the awards he had won, in order to validate his inner sense of self-worth. Now he needed to balance these factors with other ways to nurture his confidence, such as being purpose-led, feeding his creativity through reflection and reading, plus getting back into regular exercise and investing time and energy in his family.

I am a great believer that self-confidence comes about as a result of meeting certain requirements – increasing your capability; deepening your knowledge and identifying and delivering to specific targets, rather than simply applying positive thinking and telling yourself to be confident.

It is critical that you are clear as to what you need in order to build sustainable confidence and self-belief. In the absence of clarity you run the risk of chasing elusive goals or becoming reliant on external factors that do not ultimately support you and the growth of your real confidence.

Ask yourself, *What do I need in order to be truly confident?*

Try an honest assessment focusing on these 4 different levels:

1. Physical confidence

How well are you managing your physical well-being in order to have the required energy and impact you need to operate at your best? On a personal note, I recently suffered from low energy as a consequence of global travel, having young children plus a very demanding workload. I decided to begin daily exercise by getting a cross trainer and doing pilates to help shift my energy and strengthen my core; and to pay more attention to my diet. As a consequence my increased energy allows me the real chance to honour my commitments, helping me to feel better about myself, which supports my confidence.

2. Emotional confidence

Are you managing your emotional well-being so that you can feel sufficiently on top of your game? One of the greatest drains on confidence is emotional turbulence, frustration, guilt, rejection, fear, anxiety, anger, helplessness or depression. These emotions prevent you from thinking clearly, behaving constructively and keep you feeling disconnected from your purpose and values. The result of resolving emotional disturbance is to get back in touch with your inner confidence.

3. Intellectual confidence

How mindful are you in terms of incorporating new ideas in order to stimulate your creativity and innovative thinking? As a leader, it is essential to deliberately pursue intellectual challenges so that you keep raising the bar of your thinking. The best leaders I know schedule 'think days' where they shut themselves away and take time to reflect upon their internal challenges and external landscape in order to stretch their thinking.

4. Spiritual confidence

Are you managing to keep yourself truly inspired? Most leaders have not invested sufficiently in their spiritual development. Remember that a lack of clarity about your core purpose and values, why you do what you do, and the type of contribution you want to make could easily lead to a life devoid of meaning and zap your confidence.

We all have the potential to enjoy real confidence. However the level is determined by our self-awareness and willingness to take the necessary steps to prove to ourselves that we've got what it takes to be our best selves.

Take a Lead

Ask yourself: *What do I need in order to become more confident?*

Commit to 'growing' your confidence by conducting a self-assessment using the criteria of physical, emotional, intellectual and spiritual confidence and formulating an action plan based on your findings.

On a 1-10 scale (10 = very high, 1 = very low) how do you rate your:

- Physical confidence _____

- Emotional confidence _____

- Intellectual confidence _____

- Spiritual confidence _____

Where would you like to be?

What steps do you need to take to be your best self?

Great coaching draws out the brilliance in people

How can you enable people to go beyond what they think is possible?

Chapter 33

Bring Out the Best in Others

Your success as a leader largely depends on how well you develop the confidence and capabilities of others.

Most leaders will agree with this in principle, but it's far less common to find those who really excel at nurturing their employees' talents. All too often the good intent gets lost in the 'busyness' of the day, and consequently gaps appear in succession plans for developing the next generation of leaders.

The usual excuse I hear is lack of time. However, I'm convinced that this is more to do with either having the insufficient capability to develop others – or the lack of desire to do so.

The leaders I know who invest in developing their people regard it as the most rewarding part of their job – and they possess a tremendous skill set for it. Their ability is rooted in coaching and I honestly believe that every leader has the innate ability to be a great coach and get the best out of others.

We hear a lot about coaching, but what is it exactly?

The type of coaching that I'm referring to is *non-directive* coaching.

Traditionally, coaching is defined as giving instruction, providing advice or solving someone's problem. Although these are all valid approaches, the main way that you build up *self-sufficiency* in others is by helping them arrive at their own solutions.

In my book, *SuperCoaching*, co-authored with Graham Alexander, we define highly effective coaching as *'an enabling process encouraging people to go beyond what they think is possible'*.

In essence, non-directive coaching 'pulls' out of others their own ideas for resolving issues and moving swiftly into action. It is a learning model that helps people to self-reflect on the pros and cons of situations and take personal responsibility for their movement forward.

Non-directive coaching has its origins in a hypothesis formulated by Timothy Gallwey, author of *The Inner Game*. His theory: *Performance equals potential minus interference.* Gallwey worked as a tennis instructor in California in the 1960's. Initially, he focused his efforts on giving traditional instruction to his players – with mixed results. Trying another approach, he soon discovered that if he simply invited his students to focus their awareness on their strokes *simply as they were*, their technique evolved naturally and seemed to self-correct. I call it mindfulness at work. Players using Gallwey's methods improved far more rapidly than usual, and without the self-criticism or trying so hard to 'do it right'. By quieting their own self-interference, they were able to tap into their natural ability with much greater ease.

Consider the benefits of coaching people, enabling them to reduce unnecessary interference and get a far closer match between their potential and performance. I believe that most people perform at least one level down from their potential – so if one could realise even 10% more potential on a consistent basis, one would enjoy a great return from a performance perspective.

Max is one of the most effective leaders I've ever come across. His whole ethos is based on growing his people in order to grow the organisation – and he recognises that the best use of his time is in supporting his team and challenging them to go beyond what they think is possible. As a consequence, they consistently outperform their targets, are firmly in the top right-hand box of the company's talent pool and enjoy a fast career progression.

Max sets very clear expectations with his people. They contract to defined KPI's (key performance indicators) and agree the level of accountability required to deliver. From that point on, Max makes himself available for coaching as and when needed. In his formal one-to-ones with his team, he focuses less on information updates and more on the big issues at hand. He requires his team to consider the most current hot topics, which if resolved would make the biggest difference to performance, and asks them to bring them to him. Together they enter into a 'coaching conversation' in order to explore where they are and draw out solutions for moving forward.

Max is a big fan of GROW – Goal-Reality-Options-Wrap-up – the model most commonly used to facilitate coaching conversations. GROW was created by coaching mentor, Graham Alexander, and originated during a process of observation with McKinsey consultants during a training programme. Coaching is instinctive to Graham. He can have a simple conversation that will end up adding massive value to a client. McKinseys were able to take an objective viewpoint, analysing the process that Graham utilised.

The elements of GROW are:

1. Goal

First, establish the topic of conversation. It might be long-range, such as leadership development, career progression or stakeholder management. Or more immediate, such as a specific meeting, relationship or development need. Second, agree the tangible takeaway that you want as a direct result of the coaching conversation. This is usually a new idea or particular set of actions that will move you in the direction you want to go.

2. Reality

Explore what is actually happening. The purpose is to clarify what is working well in a situation, what is not working and to recognise what might be missing. It's important to keep this aspect of the process at a broad level without jumping to any early conclusions. It can be helpful to make a distinction between what's going on now – i.e. the current reality as well as what success will look like – i.e. the desired future state. Use open questions so that the conversation stays at the right level, allowing the person being coached to explore what is going on.

3. Options

This phase is all about generating new ideas in order to resolve the most critical issues on the table. It's important not to drill down too quickly into a preferred option and to generate at least half a dozen options as potential ways forward. A creative questioning approach is necessary to allow the person being coached to be open to new possibilities and think differently. It's at this part of the conversation that the temptation for the coach to jump in with their own ideas is very high. It's not wrong to give input, the 'coaching police' won't come after you, however it's essential to hold back from giving input until the other person has exhausted their own thinking. A useful challenge as coach is that if the person you are coaching dries up, rather than telling them what you think, ask a different question to open up even more options.

4. Wrap-up

The wrap-up phase is used to analyse options, decide on a preferred one or two and then agree on specific action-oriented steps to move forwards. It is vital at this stage of the conversation to explore any potential interference that may stop someone from following up on their commitments. Agree on future coaching support in order to track progress. Finally, upon completion go back and check the original goal for the session to see if success has been achieved.

Although there is a logical flow to GROW, once you have internalised the approach you will find that the most powerful coaching sessions rarely go in a linear way. As someone begins to peel the layers off the onion, new insights emerge which may require you to reset the first goal. In the Option phase, it's often the case that you need to explore reality further in order to get even more clarity about what's going on. In any case your willingness to be flexible as a coach and your ability to be comfortable with ambiguity are critical to allowing your recipient to go in the direction that's right for them.

As a leader there are two main approaches to coaching: 'on your seat coaching' and 'on your feet' coaching. The first consists of formal interaction, such as personal reviews and appraisals and the second occurs around coffee vending machines and those water cooler moments – through informal conversations when people have something on their mind they want to fix.

The main concern I hear about coaching is the amount of time it takes. There is no doubt that initially there is an investment in time – an opposite approach to the quick fix. However, in the longer term the payback is multifold as people stop coming to you with issues to resolve and start realising their own potential to take the initiative and flourish.

Performance equals potential minus interference.

Take a Lead

1. Challenge yourself to develop a coaching style which will accelerate the development of others.

2. Identify the top talent on your team who would be open to being coached and schedule time to have non-directive coaching conversations following the GROW model.

The right feedback is a gift

'I want to give you some feedback.'

Chapter 34

The Art of Feedback

It was a Saturday morning, the sun was shining and I was out playing with my kids in the park, pushing them on the swings, when my phone suddenly pinged with a work text. It is extremely rare that I let myself get involved with work during the weekends, however the message caused me concern. A client was threatening to leave his job after having received feedback from his boss on his way home from work the previous evening.

I quickly called him back to see if we could nip the issue in the bud. As I heard what had happened, I got a feeling of dread. Tony's line manager had called him to give him 'feedback' about a presentation he'd delivered to the Board earlier in the day, the gist of it being: *'You were not at your best today. In fact you always appear nervous with the Board. It comes across that you are not committed to your role and that your engagement is low. They are losing faith in you.'*

I could understand why he was on the verge of quitting.

I suggested that before making any rash moves we should explore the data in more detail. First, had his line manager ever given him feedback previously about his Board presentations? No, and therefore my client had assumed he was doing a good job and meeting expectations. Second, had his line manager made any other references to his commitment and engagement levels in the past? Again this was new news, and unaccompanied by specific examples, had come across as random and unhelpful. Through a couple of further short questions my client was able to recognise that maybe the problem lay in the quality of the feedback. While he was completely willing to learn and grow as needed, unless he received specific, evidence-based feedback that was both timely and constructive then it simply became a negative experience.

'I want to give you some feedback.'

How do you feel when you hear these words?

The worst type of feedback that I have come across in organisations – and no doubt you have too – is one way, from the top down, not specific enough, untimely, laden with emotion, usually associated with failure and lacking in awareness as to its impact.

We all have blind spots. But great leaders constantly seek feedback to close any gap between their version of reality and that of others. Sadly, it is rare to come across a leader who really excels at *giving* effective feedback. I believe that this is usually due to a lack of skill rather than poor intent. To give feedback well, and in the way that it can be taken on board, we need to shift the way we define it. It should be a two-way process, a sharing of information that either highlights a success, or area where current performance is outstanding and provides a clear explanation about why this is the case – or focusing on an area for improvement to help build the necessary awareness, skill set and confidence in order for someone to grow.

Below are 3 key reasons for giving useful feedback:

1. Confidence

Confidence equals capacity. In other words, if we *believe* that we can do something, we are halfway to making it possible. Therefore, a prime purpose of feedback is to build confidence in another. Ask yourself, *To what extent do I build or destroy confidence in the feedback I give?* I have seen high performers in organisations crash and burn through receiving ineffective or damaging feedback. I once had the unfortunate experience of coaching someone who had been positioned as a top talent in one particular company: Carol had progressed fast and received highly encouraging feedback along the way. However, under the leadership of a new manager she exited the company within a few months – going form hero to zero overnight. She had received feedback from her manager, but it destroyed her as it was personal, non-specific and led to no possible constructive options.

2. Ownership

If a person receiving feedback fails to take ownership of an issue nothing will change, therefore it is the responsibility of the leader who gives feedback to ensure that ownership *can* take place. On one occasion I had to debrief a client with some tricky messages from management. Even though I expressed it in the most palatable of ways he blew up at me as if the information had come from me. Yet, I was simply the messenger. It took several weeks of reflection and further conversations in order for him to accept and own the feedback as valuable data that would make a real difference if acted upon.

3. Action

A primary reason for a sceptical attitude regarding feedback is that often people fail to do anything with the information they are given. The number of times I hear leaders saying upon receiving feedback, *Oh I've heard this all before*, or *There's nothing new here*, as if that were something to be proud of. One of the most important aspects of giving feedback is to *help* someone act upon it, otherwise two things will happen: your interest in giving feedback will wane and your people's progress will be compromised.

After understanding these reasons, the following 4 key steps will ensure that the feedback you give is not only useful but can be acted upon:

A. Relationship

Before offering feedback you need to ask yourself, *Is there a strong enough relationship base for me to provide feedback?* If not, either due to insufficient time having been spent together, or something more significant such as a lack of trust, then your feedback won't be heard and the process could backfire. Sometimes I come across leaders who think that giving feedback is a way of building relationship. This is not the case. It's essential that you have invested enough time and energy in the relationship bank account first, before moving on to feedback.

B. Intention

When it comes to giving feedback what is your real intent? For only when you have the right intention to support and challenge are you are in the position to provide clear and candid feedback. Be aware that unless your intent is *genuinely* wanting to help someone grow and fulfill their potential, it is highly unlikely that they will receive your feedback in a constructive way no matter how accurate it is. Some fascinating research in the field of social intelligence shows how we are literally wired up to pick up on the intent of others. Daniel Goleman writes in *The Neural Power of Leadership* that: *'Mirror neurons are a kind of "neural wi-fi" that monitor what is happening in other people. This system tracks their emotions, what movements they're making, what they intend and it activates, in our brains, precisely the same brain areas as are active in the other person. This puts us on the same wavelength and it does it automatically, instantaneously and unconsciously.'*

C. Emotion

If you are feeling angry or frustrated about someone's behaviour, and dress your feedback up to disguise your emotion, the recipient will pick up on the underlying feeling and will fail to hear the real data in the feedback. My wife is a master at picking up on my real feelings, so there's no chance of masking something with sugar coating. She will not let me off the hook until I've shared how I feel as well as what I wanted to say. Depending on what relationship or situation you find yourself in, it's essential to either process your own emotions so that you can give feedback in a way that the recipient can hear, or to make a clear distinction between the facts and your feelings, for instance saying: *'When this happened I felt…'* It is essential that you take ownership of how you feel so that there is no projection or blame on others.

D. Information

There is nothing more frustrating than being given feedback without specific examples and evidence to explain the point. For instance, being told 'you are always late,' is not very helpful until you have given actual examples of when you were late, by how much, how often and the impact of being late. Personally, I find the best way of managing information is to have it written down so that during the conversation there is an evidence base to work from, rather than recalling incidents under pressure.

Consider these six levels of feedback, going from least to most effective:

Level 1: Personal Criticism

At its lowest form feedback is biting criticism. Here little, if any, responsibility is taken for a point of view and un-backed by factual evidence. Unhelpful criticism is driven by a desire on the giver's part to be right; it is filled with blame and achieves nothing but ill feeling. An example is telling someone that they perform poorly, without any data to substantiate it. It destroys confidence and says more about the ineffectuality of the giver than the receiver.

Level 2: Generalised Judgment

Generalisations are never helpful. For instance, telling someone that they do not add value during meetings is a sure way to take the stuffing out of them and give them a piece of information they can't do anything with. Or remarking that a PowerPoint presentation, which was obviously done with care, isn't displaying the right information, when there had been no prior and specific agreement about the content.

Level 3: Specific Judgment

The trouble with judging someone is that it simply switches them off. For example, telling one of your team that their interpersonal skills leave a lot to be desired, not only puts their back up but runs the risk of generating no ownership in the recipient which becomes extremely demotivating. It is surprising how much people want to improve if given a helpful critique where there is room to grow.

Level 4: Generalised Self–assessment

We're now moving up to a point where feedback will encourage ownership, but may fail to move someone into action. Generalised self-assessment starts with asking how someone views their own performance, thus helping to raise awareness and creating a two-way exchange of information before giving feedback. You could ask, *What worked well in the presentation you gave? What didn't work as well? What would you do differently next time?* In this way you get a clear sense of their own self-assessment before sharing your observations.

Level 5: Focused Self–assessment

This is the highest level of feedback and based on strong relationship, a clear intent to help someone learn and grow, appropriate emotion and specific information. It starts by drawing out of the recipient their initial reflections about a situation, including clarity as to their intent, the facts of what happened and what they would do differently next time. For instance, asking such questions as: *What outcome did you want to achieve? How did you think you performed against this outcome? What did you do that moved the agenda forward? What did you do to cause any interference? What would you think of doing differently next time?*

Level 6: Finally, Feedback

In providing your feedback, make sure that you own your observations, and use the 'I' point of view when speaking directly to the recipient. For example, *During your presentation I thought you did a great job engaging the audience through your use of eye contact, humour and specific examples. I encourage you to speak 10% more slowly, breathe in between sentences and summarise your message into 3 clear points upon completion to add even more impact.* It's clear, simple and allows someone to act upon it if they wish to.

The concept 'feedback is a gift' has become somewhat of a cliché in business, however great leaders are constantly hungry for feedback, seeking it on a regular basis and making sure they become known for giving it. The benefit is huge in terms of closing the gap between how you think you're performing and how others perceive it – allowing you to establish an accurate picture of how you lead.

Take a Lead

Rate yourself on the following scale (1 = never, 10 = always):

1. I ensure that my relationships are in the right place before I offer feedback:

2. My intent is to help others grow and fulfill their potential:

3. I take ownership of my feelings so that they are not projected onto others:

4. I provide specific and evidence-based information so that others can clearly understand my observations:

Getting to the truth

I recommend senior leaders to go through a '360-feedback'
process every 24 months.

Chapter 35

360-feedback

What is 360-feedback? Simply put, it is a process of collecting and organising data from a carefully selected range of sources, such as one's line manager, direct reports and peers – followed by a debriefing.

360-feedback allows for the unique opportunity of getting confidential views on your effectiveness as a leader and is one of the most helpful and enlightening methods I have found in over 20 years of work.

Thankfully, this procedure is now common practice in most organisations.

I recommend senior leaders to go through a 360-feedback every 24 months. Or, if someone has started a new role you could bring this down to a yearly exercise. Often the 360-feedback tool is a generic set of questions based on the desired leadership competencies in the company. While this allows for good insights, the most valuable 360-feedback tools are those personally designed by the leader himself and based on the question, 'What do you want to know about yourself?' This generates immediate ownership when the feedback is received, as it is what the leader specified what he or she wanted to focus on. The next step is to nominate who they want feedback drawn from, taking a well-rounded selection of people – upwards, sideways and downwards as well as both internal and external to the organisation, including some respondents with whom they do not see eye to eye.

In my experience, the best type of 360-feedback is qualitative data. Of course it is useful to have a selection of quantitative questions too, but people often become distracted by numbers and fail to pay sufficient attention to the meaning in the comments.

Some of my favourite questions are the following:

- How would you describe 'Joe' in 5 words or less?
- What does he do when at his very best?
- What specifically does he do that inspires and engages?
- What value does he bring to the business?
- What is his definition of success?
- How clearly does he define success for others?
- How well does he communicate success?
- How well does he recognise and celebrate success?
- What does he do that inhibits or demotivates you?
- What are his key development themes?
- What could he do differently to support and challenge your performance to raise your game?
- How would you rate the coaching support he provides?
- How effective is he in giving you valuable feedback?
- How collaborative is he in the way he works with you and others?
- What does the organisation need most from him going forward?
- What should he stop, start and continue doing to be the best he can be?

Once I've had the opportunity to interview nominees first hand, usually about twelve people, I organise the data and write up a detailed report – a combination of key themes supported by direct verbatim comments to substantiate the insights.

On one occasion, a key strength that emerged after asking what value a leader added to her organisation was: 'demonstrates great credibility'. This insight was supported by comments such as, '*Has a degree of wisdom. Commands huge trust and respect from the business community. Seen by the vast majority of colleagues as a confident, measured and successful leader who looks and talks the part. Hugely aware of the importance of doing and saying the right thing. She fulfills her leadership shoes.*'

Contrast this with the development themes of another leader: 'needs to have a more flexible leadership style'. The comments that related to this included, '*Not as politically savvy as he could be. Tends to talk too much. Uses 'I' rather than 'we' statements. Doesn't allow others the opportunity to discuss.*'

Once I've collected the feedback and written up a report – but before handing it over the leader – I ask them the same set of questions in order to get an honest self-assessment. On one occasion a highly self-aware leader accurately described himself to the word in terms of both his leadership strengths and development areas. He had a favourite mantra that symbolised his leadership style, '*Tight, loose, tight*'. However he recognised that his recent style was in fact, '*Tight, tight, tight*'. He was micro-managing and knew it.

Following the self-assessment, I then give my client the report and try to capture their initial reactions in the form of any successes, surprises or disappointments. We then go through the report in depth and synthesise the most important areas for consideration. I give the client the opportunity to seek clarification on any of the points, however I do not breach any confidence as to the specific source of comments. *This is crucial.* Although it's tempting for the client to try and identify where comments came from, I challenge them to not go down this route, but to stay very focused on the overall themes.

A reflection period of 3-5 days is then agreed on for the leader to re-read the report, respond to the initial findings and then choose two or three specific themes that they will incorporate into their development going forward. These may be leadership strengths to build upon, as well as gaps in their abilities. We will then work together to formalise an action plan to set in motion addressing these themes. I tend to use three main areas for an action plan, i.e. *What does success look like, Key enablers* and *Specific actions.*

One example focusing on strategic thinking included:

	Development Theme – Be a great Strategic Thinker
What does success look like?	• Being recognised across the business for my thoughtful insight and engaging way of sharing ideas • Having my line manager and team members appreciate my thought leadership and my ability to articulate new ideas clearly and simply • Making connections across the organisation to create shared insight • Being the conscience in conversations for focusing on the big picture

Key enablers	• Structured thinking to build insight about the business agenda • Visit other departments and regions to understand other approaches • Mentoring from a great strategic thinker
Specific actions	• To validate my development plan with line manager, mentor and peer support • To confirm and agree mentoring programme • To read one article a month on strategic thinking • To schedule monthly visits to a department or region and set up thought-provoking meetings • To schedule a monthly 'think day' to review and progress my strategic agenda

I always track progress closely in order to encourage real momentum to occur. It's very rewarding when leaders take giant strides forward based on 360 development data so that 24 months later, what comes through in the next set of findings is the recognition and appreciation of their commitment to focus and grow.

Take a Lead

Ask yourself:

- What do I want to know about myself?

- Who do I want feedback from?

- Decide on approximately 12 key questions and 12 nominations.

- Ideally have a 3rd party (coach or trusted advisor) to complete the interviews.

Alternatively, create your own anonymous survey (register with Survey Monkey) and do it online.

If you don't grow, others won't grow

The hardest work we do is the work on ourselves.

Chapter 36

Plan to Grow

Each year I decide on an overarching theme for that year – something I need to focus on that I want to develop, need or am lacking in.

This year my word is TRUST.

It helps me focus on my inner journey and by 'growing myself' makes a massive difference to the quality of my work, life and relationships.

I would now cite the focus of one central personal theme for a year as best practice for 'growing yourself'.

Several years ago, somewhat at the beginning of my career, I was invited to run a leadership programme in Dubai for the CEO of a company. Alec had one real passion – personal development – and he believed that in order for a company to grow, its leaders must grow too.

He was determined to make personal development a key priority for his senior leaders, whom he believed had never before had the opportunity really focus on their own growth. Alec was a planner at heart, and from his operational experience knew that unless his leaders had thoughtful personal development plans (PDPs) then what he was aspiring to would fail.

He asked for my help in with designing a session to ensure that his leaders created meaningful PDPs.

A challenging assignment! Mostly because the majority of PDPs I had come across in organisations up to that point were not worth the paper they were written on.

People simply completed them to meet corporate requirements without putting any real thought into their development. The responses were tactical, overly focused on career progression involving technical skills, and had far too many targets to ever be accomplished in a year. As a consequence, they tended to get dusted down twice a year during the performance management cycle and the evolution of somebody's PDP was a copy-and-paste exercise, duplicating the points of the previous year.

I had never devised a PDP for my own growth. I didn't report to anyone and I had never been a great fan of structure – but if I was going to run a session about it, I challenged myself to create my own personal development plan so that I could speak authentically about the subject. I established seven key must do's:

1. Focus

Each year, a leader must have one overarching development theme to focus on. There can be subsets of this theme, but if you focus on one thing and commit to mastering it in a year you will enjoy the most meaningful growth.

2. Inspiration

Does your personal development theme inspire you? If not, you will struggle to keep it alive. To have the most impact and effect, it must pull you in the direction you want to *grow* in.

3. Stretch

The theme must take you out of your comfort zone as you only grow when you're being challenged to think and do things differently.

4. Measurement

You must create clear success criteria in order to track progress.

5. Action

Your PDP must be broken down into specific actions so that you can grow on a daily basis.

6. Support

You cannot grow on your own. You must identify the key people to support, challenge and hold you accountable to your word.

7. Follow up

You must follow through passionately on your commitments to accelerate your growth. If you don't take full responsibility for your development you can't expect anyone else to.

Armed with this insight, I set about creating my own PDP. In order to find my key theme, I reflected on what my greatest weakness at that time was. Defaulting to other people's point of view. I decided that WISDOM would be my theme. I had always resonated with the symbol of the North Star as an image to inspire my growth so I used it as my focal point. I backed up my choice with acknowledging the areas which would be most impacted by developing my capability to understand, listen to and follow my inner wisdom. These were CREATIVITY, INSPIRATION, TRUST and SERVICE.

Inspiration

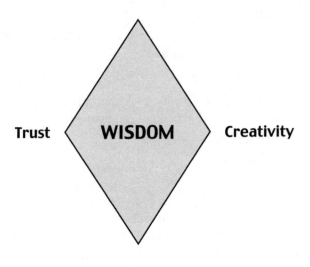

Service

To get an idea of my plan, I charted the following:

Theme	Success criteria
WISDOM	• Understand what wisdom means, how to access and utilise it to do the right thing • Be inspired by trusting and acting upon wisdom • Increase creative output by drawing upon wisdom as a guide • Be known as a trusted advisor with clients through demonstrating wise practice
Key actions	**Support**
1. Read extensively on the subject of wisdom 2. Engage role models to follow 3. Speak up in meetings 4. Rely on own research rather than defaulting to others	1. Coach 2. Mentor 3. Business partners

As a consequence of my PDP I enjoyed the most accelerated growth I'd had in years and the benefits swept the board. I created far more impactful development programmes for clients, my writing became clearer and more decisive, and I grew in confidence and capability to deliver presentations. The icing on the cake was when I attended an end of year client event. It was held in Winchester Cathedral and had a medieval theme; during the dinner, I was touched and amused to see that my place card had 'Sir Fount of Knowledge' written on it.

Back to Dubai and the session I was running. I took the group of senior leaders through my methodology and approach, getting pretty personal and explaining the meaning a PDP had in my own life. It was a new concept for them. The majority admitted that although they were meticulous planners in their business they hadn't applied the same principles to their own personal development.

Their initial challenge was to decide on an overarching theme to focus on.

I asked for a volunteer to demonstrate the process on.

Ralph, a bright and younger-than-usual senior leader, stepped forwards. I asked him to reflect upon the biggest challenges he was facing. He shared that in his own life he took big risks and made smart decisions. But in his business practice he had the tendency to procrastinate, which delayed progress. As we continued to dig he confessed that he didn't trust the support of his team around him. He was visibly flustered talking about it, but once the issue was on the table he relaxed. The turning point in the coaching session took place when I asked him what the differentiating factor was between his work and life that resulted in him being at his best *outside* work. He said it came down to his support structure. In his life, he felt highly supported by his family, and this enabled him to take calculated risks. By the same token, it was support issues at work that derailed him.

I pointed out to the group that as a leader you are only as good as the support structure you have, so Ralph recognised that support should be his overarching development theme for the year. He went on to create a detailed personal development plan, ensured a new alignment with his line manager, and wrote to me some months later that his growth had indeed accelerated as a result.

Some other examples of overarching themes with success criteria that other leaders focused on:

AUTHENTICITY
- Focus on what's true in my work, life and relationships
- Share a compelling story to inspire and engage others
- Demonstrate balanced judgment in my decision making
- Lead with purpose and values
- Nurture my home life

ENERGY
- Be purpose-led
- Live my values
- Commit to my vision
- Be relationship orientated
- Trust my intuition

COURAGE
- Change the way we do things around here
- Be inspired to inspire others
- Push boundaries to build relationships
- See the bigger picture where my family is concerned

FREEDOM
- Re-ignite hunger for learning and growth
- Unleash passion for success
- Strengthen self-belief and confidence
- Make the right choices based on 'no fear' principle

I took the idea of the overarching theme into my own family during our winter holiday in Israel at the end of last year. We were down at the Dead Sea, when spontaneously over breakfast one morning, I asked each member of my family to name a word showing what they wanted for themselves in the coming year.

My wife declared ENJOYMENT to be hers, after a particularly challenging year. My teenage daughter decided that CONNECT would be her main theme – wanting to connect with her self, her close friends and her environment in a different way. My 7-year old son chose HAPPINESS, which for him meant having fun and being kind to others; and my four-year-old chose PLAY – which seemed pretty perfect. Mine came up as TRUST. It adds another dimension to family life when you consciously focus on your development together.

Creating a thoughtful PDP gives you the framework to accelerate your development: by consciously choosing what to focus on and how to achieve it. If you are really committed to choosing ONE overarching theme per year for the rest of your life, I guarantee that you will enjoy spectacular personal growth.

As Kirk Kinsell, President of the Americas for IHG puts it, 'The hardest work we do is the work we do on ourselves.'

Take a Lead

Decide on your overarching personal development theme to focus on.

Reflect upon recent feedback you have received to give you an indication of what development areas would make the biggest difference.

Use the following 5 questions to test your choice:

1. What would energise me the most?

2. What would stretch me the furthest?

3. What strength can I build upon?

4. What would challenge me to think differently?

5. What would inspire me to grow?

Write up your PDP based on a version of the following framework:

- Development theme
- What success will look like
- Key actions to take
- Timing
- Who will be involved

Winning teams

The true test of a leader is the quality of the team you build.

Chapter 37

Lead your Team

Leaders succeed or fail on the strength of their teams.

Simple.

If you, as a leader, build a winning team you set yourself up for success. If you don't, you won't. Interestingly, the majority of leaders I coach say that their true fulfillment lies in leading a team of high performers, who are fully committed to each other's success in all aspects of work and life – the benefits of creating a top team go way beyond business performance.

Through coaching numerous high-performance teams I have identified 7 key characteristics, and 'must do's' for a winning team: *Clear Purpose, Shared Values, Aligned Vision & Strategy, Deep Trust, Deliver on Promises, Personal Growth* and *Celebrate Success.*

1. Clear Purpose

A dysfunctional team is one made up of individuals who demonstrate silo ways of working. While I haven't yet met anyone who wakes up in the morning with the deliberate intent to exclude others from their world, I am convinced that this happens due to a lack of shared common purpose.

A clear purpose is the glue that binds a team together. It gives a team its raison d'etre. A well defined purpose becomes the team's heartbeat – over and above the simple meeting of objectives. As leadership guru Peter Drucker states: *'The best preparation for a smooth journey, even as we steer across troubled waters or leap across chasms, is a clear sense of meaningful purpose.'* The methodology I use to help a team define its purpose is to explore its desired future state. I start in the early stages of a team's formation, and revisit 'the purpose' on a frequent basis to ensure that it is still relevant, being acted upon and adding value.

STEP 1

Get each team member to write down five adjectives about how they would like to see the team in a year's time. Typically, these words are aspirational as the team is in its formative stages and does not yet embody them. Examples of adjectives include: inspirational, winning, collaborative, top-performing, fun, supportive, trusting and respectful.

STEP 2

Each member shares their list and sees how many words the team has in common. This is a powerful moment for seeing the level of alignment in the team, as there are usually only 1 or 2 adjectives that people have in common. Also, the descriptions represent what's most important for each person and give the first glimpse as to where they are coming from.

STEP 3

You now bring the words together and have the team vote on their top three. The real value of this part of the process is for the team to have the conversation about what they want to stand for.

STEP 4

You can now summarise the findings into a 'team purpose statement'. Take some examples from previous teams I have coached:

> *Inspiring people to be the best they can be in order to deliver an excellent service.*
> – Operational Leadership Team

> *To be a trusted partner in the business helping drive a highly engaged workforce to improve customer experience.*
> – HR Leadership Team

> *Inspiring love.*
> – Global Communications Team

Getting clear on a purpose is not a wordsmith exercise. The real value is that it takes a team on a journey of understanding what lies at the heart and soul of its identity.

2. Shared Values

Values are a team's lifeblood, and provide a code for consistent behaviour. In the absence of clearly identified and owned values there is no framework for people to measure what 'good' looks like in terms of their own behaviour. The process of defining shared values is a powerful exercise for bringing a team together and enables team members to understand how they can work together in the future.

One way I like to support a team in articulating its values is by asking people what they may be able to bring to the table from previous winning teams they've been a part of – what values were demonstrated which they saw had inspired greatness?

Once, a team member spoke about having taken part in delivering a vital aspect of the London 2012 Olympics. His team had had to perform a herculean task in order for the Olympic body to run to plan, and were under extreme time pressure to do so. At a crucial moment, rather than pressing on with their task list, they stepped back to define their shared values – knowing that it would give them the required clarity to work best together. They came up with the following set of values:

- Be authentic
- Do the right thing
- Work better together
- Encourage others to be their best selves
- Create sustainable success

This gave them a shared platform to support and challenge each other in living these values in the run up to, and during, the Games. It allowed them to have difficult conversations because everyone knew the real intent behind what was being said. It enabled them to be fearless in their approach to each other. And it gave them the right context for making decisions and unlocking the potential of the team. They measured themselves against their stated values using a 1-10 scale to see how effectively they were living them, and then kept raising the bar to ensure that they were consistent in their approach.

3. Aligned Vision & Strategy

It never ceases to amaze me how hard teams can work without having aligned on what success looks like. Given the amount of time, energy and resource that goes into delivering a vision, one of the most critical stages of team development is to ensure everyone is on the same page in terms of the big picture. A savvy leader must involve his or her team in the process of creating both its vision and strategic priorities, otherwise they will run the risk of the team paying lip service through not having been given sufficient ownership.

Creating a shared vision is not a straightforward process and requires several iterations before a team is genuinely aligned in the right direction.

I once coached a global team that had limited time together. As a consequence it became even more important to clarify what success looked like for them in order to be as effective as possible. The organisation had a 3-year planning cycle so we used that as the timeline for the vision. We set up a creative conversation for people to dream up what they wanted to be famous for in 3 years' time. The team identified several key areas at the heart of the vision including the development of its people, the quality of its brand, the innovation of its product line and the impact on its environment. On the back of this picture we were able to define the key strategic priorities that could bring their vision to life.

Detailed action plans were set up to support the delivery of the priorities, which were then periodically reviewed. At year-end, we conducted a full review on where their vision 'stood' and refreshed it accordingly.

I always encourage the leader of a team to take a highly collaborative approach in the journey of creating a vision and strategy in order to generate full buy-in and ownership. However if there are some non-negotiable themes that the leader wants to include they must be clear and direct about them. There is nothing worse than a leader compromising on what they believe, as it will only cause conflict down the road.

4. Deep Trust

Trust is the magical ingredient that makes all the other characteristics of a high performing team possible. In the absence of trust everything is simply an academic exercise. Yes, you need a purpose. Yes, you need a vision and strategy. However, if there is limited trust then the team will simply not work together in an effective way. Conversations will be stilted; people will not speak their minds; feelings will be hidden; behaviour becomes underhand. A lack of trust breeds an even greater lack of trust. As Stephen Covey stated in his eye-opening article, 'How the Best Leaders Build Trust': *When trust is low, in a company or in a relationship, it places a hidden 'tax' on every transaction: every communication, every interaction, every strategy, every decision is taxed, bringing speed down and sending costs up. My experience is that significant distrust doubles the cost of doing business and triples the time it takes to get things done.*

It's easy to talk about trust, but by the time most leaders have joined a senior team they have enough reasons to be cynical. Broken promises, failed dreams, individualistic ways of working are all common experiences that could make anyone sceptical about fostering deep trust on a team. The starting point for a team to build trust is through the example set by the leader. I once coached a team that had been through a very difficult period in which the long-term leader had left, various members of the team had applied and been rejected as his successor, and finally a new leader had been appointed. Ahead of my workshop I interviewed the team to get their reactions about how they thought the team was going to come together given the history. It didn't look good. People were planning their exit strategies. All eyes were on the new leader and they weren't particularly friendly.

I carefully debriefed the incoming leader with this non-attributable feedback from the team and she quickly got that the workshop was going to be a defining moment in either establishing trust or going bust. We agreed to use the technique of sharing personal life stories as a genuine step in building mutual trust. During the workshop, each team member was required to share the three most defining moments that had shaped their life so far, the conclusions they drew from these experiences and how they had informed their values and personal purpose. Everyone had ten minutes to tell his or her story. This exercise became a moment of truth. The leader went first and set the tone with a high degree of openness and honesty. The team showed great appreciation for the level of disclosure and reciprocated by also showing real courage by taking the rest of the team into their confidence.

The following were some of the comments from team members as a result of the session:

'The raw honesty and confidence that people felt that they could share very personal events in their life demonstrated the real comfort that the team felt with one another. It was almost as if we had been plunged into some form of crisis that we had to manage our way out of. Whilst the team are entrenched in their respective work streams, the collective process required to deliver our objectives is now underwritten by a shared trust amongst the team.'

'The objective of the session was to create a high performing team which could create a transformational change in the business in terms of performance and people engagement. The investment of telling our stories helped to drive a significantly different leadership approach to engagement, performance and collaboration and delivered the desired outcome to

operate in a vastly different way. The 'giving of ourselves' was the foundation to achieving it.'

'We significantly accelerated our performance from the perspective of task and team through building trust stronger than any team I've worked in.'

5. Deliver on Promises

The natural extension of deep trust is to deliver on your promises. There is nothing more damaging to the reputation of a team – or the relationships within it – than people making and breaking commitments. No matter what people say, unless promises are evidenced through tangible deliverables and expectations clearly managed if there is to be late or non-delivery, then credibility will be seriously compromised.

When I coach a team I make it very clear that I would much rather people say that they are not going to deliver on their commitments rather than to nod heads, only to walk out of the room and do nothing. Delivering on promises is a clear mark of respect and, by the same token, not delivering shows a lack thereof. No team can afford undermined respect. Having said that I haven't come across anyone who goes out of their way to not deliver (call me naive). Instead, I genuinely believe that if delivery is not taking place, then there is some kind of interference that needs to be identified, understood and removed. It may be the setting of unrealistic targets, having a lack of capability and resource, or not having sufficient alignment about ways of working.

One of the most effective teams I had the privilege of coaching set up a simple system to support them in their target delivery – at the mid-point of a financial year the leader took stock, only to discover that the team was not managing. He moved quickly, pulling the team together to collectively devise a plan, which gave greater visibility vis a vis their desired targets, ensuring that everyone had direct accountability for a joint delivery. They put in very specific work streams against each deliverable with clear timelines, and a programme management office to measure progress. Within weeks, results began to shift as the rigour and focus kicked in. As a consequence of delivering on promises, the team were highly energised and their success infectious, spreading to all those they came in contact with.

6. Personal Growth

A winning team consists of a group of high-performance individuals who are dedicated to both their *own* personal development as well as the growth and development of their fellow team members. In fact, often the most meaningful aspect of a team is when there is the opportunity to accelerate the development of those on the team, or those impacted by the team. Winning teams embody this fundamental concept: *In order for a team to grow, its people need to grow.*

However, personal development is often the vital missing part of a team working together. It is rare indeed to come across a team that puts individual growth on the agenda and can support and challenge each other to grow.

To facilitate this, one of my favourite exercises is creating the opportunity – and safe space – for team members to give each other candid feedback about what they 1) appreciate about each other and 2) would encourage each other to do more of in order to accelerate their forward growth.

Of course this exercise is usually met with resistance. Yet, almost without exception, everyone claims it to be the highlight of the day, as they learn so much about themselves as well as deepening their relationships with others. It's not an easy process as often the feedback received can be difficult to take on board, however when it's given with the right intent, to help each other grow, then it propels people to new heights.

Another valuable process is for team members to share where they are on their own leadership journeys, in particular which key personal development themes they are focused on at the moment. One leader I coached was passionate about doing this, and – usually over a good dinner with some fine wine – would hold an annual get together so that each team member could know where everyone else stood in terms of their career and personal aspirations.

Mac led the evening by speaking openly about what he was up against, including the challenges he faced with his line manager, the school choices he was having to make for his kids, the financial goals for his family's support, and creative input that he needed to perform at his best. This experience deeply bonded his team, ensuring that they were clear about what success looked like for themselves, their future development and strengthened their commitment to supporting each other along the way.

7. Celebrate Success

It's astonishing how often teams can forget to recognise, talk about, learn from and celebrate their success. We slog along the path to success and then forget to reward ourselves and each other when we get there. But when we do, the benefits are enormous and multifaceted. Increased energy. Sharing of best practice. Having a sense of pride. Enjoying the journey.

What I'm talking about here is an authentic way of making success a learning curve and genuinely appreciating the efforts of others. If we do not celebrate our success, team morale drops, individualistic behaviour takes over, a transactional attitude prevails and there is limited personal development.

George was a master at both recognising and celebrating his team's successes. He was a great believer in the benefits of playing full out as a team. I have had some of my most memorable team coaching experiences spending time with his various teams.

Once, overlooking scenic Barcelona from a hotel balcony, while his team gave and received feedback to each other based on their personal contributions that year. Another time, after a fantastic water volleyball game in Tuscany on a retreat which he organised to thank his team for another successful year.

However, celebrating success does not have to be an expensive affair.

You can start a team meeting by recognising recent successes which you have achieved together, defining the key enablers for achieving that success, and clarifying what you can build upon in the future. Bringing to light a team's successes invigorates them and raises their energy and desire for a future success-focused culture.

Building a winning team is the very real result of winning leadership.

Take a Lead

If you are leading a team, conduct a mini-team audit by asking the team to rate itself on a scale of 1-10 (1 = very low, 10 = very high) against the following dimensions:

1. Having a clear purpose

2. Living shared values

3. Following an aligned vision and strategy

4. Building deep trust

5. Delivering promises

6. Encouraging personal growth

7. Celebrating success

If you score less than 8 on any area, work out together how you can improve going forward to reach 9 or 10/10.

No reflection, no leadership

Reflection is one of the most powerful leadership
muscles we can develop.

Chapter 38

Time to Reflect

Traditionally, we associate leadership with being very action-oriented: setting strategy, leading presentations, running meetings and making decisions.

Right?

Although this is true to an extent, what makes the difference between the *good* and *great* leader is the degree that you reflect on what's most important before moving into action.

One of the top leaders I know is hugely committed to the practice of reflection. Adrian recently became Managing Director of one of the largest retail companies in the UK, and invited me to run his first 'team-build' event, which was to bring together an extremely talented group of leaders. I encouraged him to devote the best part of the first morning to sharing what he stood for as a leader simply in order for his new team could get to know him, and see where he was coming from.

Adrian invested a considerable amount of time reflecting upon what he would say.

He talked about his passion for freedom which stemmed from his love of new ideas and people, his unconventional approach and his enjoyment of creativity and change. He also talked about the importance of relationship. Adrian is extremely committed to his family and close circle of friends. Because his joy lies in the connection he experiences with people, many of his professional relationships become genuine friendships. He also has a strong faith, which provides sustenance and support during challenging times. As a consequence of the time he took to reflect on his leadership, his team greatly appreciated the insight they gained, agreeing that one morning had saved them several months of trying to figure out their new boss.

Let's contrast this with Trevor, another leader I've worked with, who is reluctant to take time to reflect. Trevor is a great strategic thinker who is happy making big decisions and communicating them to the world. However, he fails to give sufficient attention to his inner motivations. On one occasion I witnessed a major fall out with one of his most important clients as a consequence of his failure to tune into *their* world. Trevor attempted to make a change to a strategic investment that would have a big impact on the client, without having diligently computed the implications of the forward motion of this move.

Needless to say, it backfired.

His client was furious and refused to continue. Trevor had to back-pedal fast to undo the damage.

The benefit of the experience? It forced him to reflect, and to deepen his understanding about the importance of engaging others.

Although many people get the concept of time for reflection, it's much harder to put it into practice. What does it actually mean?

Let's take a practical example. I once coached Fiona, a senior leader, in preparation for the company annual end-of-year conference with her 250 top leaders. It had been a tough year from a trading perspective, and Fiona was ready to put across a tough message. Her goal was to have people feel the pain of missing targets in order to get them to take greater accountability for the year ahead.

I asked her why she was taking this approach, only to be amazed by her answer. She hadn't really thought about it!

So after asking her a few leading questions to help her reflect, such, as *What does success look like regarding this meeting? What do you want people to understand and feel as a result of her message? How did she want to be perceived?* Fiona decided to change her tack.

How?

She depicted a compelling story about what her leaders had been through together and how she needed their help in going forward to move performance to top notch. Fiona became more emotionally honest about how she felt about the year and her own leadership. The feedback from the group was the best she had ever received. They warmed to her vulnerability, appreciated her empathy and were inspired by her honesty. But most significant? The top 250 went on to lead the organsation the following year to their most impressive set of results.

When I followed up with Fiona some months later, and asked her about the turning point in performance, she said without hesitation that having taken the necessary time to reflect at that crucial moment had enabled her to change her approach, and be far more in-tune with the needs of her people.

Reflection is one of the most powerful leadership muscles you can develop. I often see leaders falling into the trap of *talking* about the importance of reflection without carving out the precious time to do it.

I would go as far as saying, 'no reflection, no leadership.' Think about the price you pay for failing to reflect. These are a few examples of what not to do:

- Not defining what 'good' looks like before moving to action.
- Not focusing on what is most important in order to stay on track.
- Not investing sufficient emotional energy in building relationships.
- Not identifying and learning from best practice.
- Not recognising and celebrating success.

It doesn't matter what type of reflection you do. So long as it is thoughtful. What is important is that you build it into your schedule. These activities can help set the scene: reading, listening to music, going for a walk, keeping a journal, exercising, meditating, conversing or any other method that works for you. When reflection becomes a natural way of life then you know you have the license to lead. In the absence of reflection, you walk on thin ice that could crack at any point.

Take a Lead

Decide on the most appropriate activity that helps you reflect, and schedule in at least 5 minutes each day until it becomes a habit.

Less a technique and more a way of being

Watch your mind and it will set you free.

Chapter 39

Mindfulness

When I was sixteen, my family went through a turbulent time. My parents were working through difficulties in their marriage, which ended up with their separation, and it prompted me to ask those big questions, like: *Why are we here? What is the point of existence? What do I really want?*

We had a holiday home in the north of England near Harrogate, more famous for its spa waters than mindfulness techniques, but one day my mother found out about an introductory talk on Transcendental Meditation and I went along with her.

We entered a room filled with businessmen. This struck me as intriguing, as I was expecting a more Eastern look instead of Western suits. I decided to stay open-minded and spent the next hour or so transfixed by the stories people told, and learning about the simple meditation technique, using a mantra, to be practised twice a day. The speakers backed up their methodology with scientific data, showing the health benefits of meditation which included lower blood pressure, deep relaxation and increased concentration. I remember making a mental note that as soon as I got to London as a student, I would learn to meditate.

I stayed true to my word, and by then aged nineteen, enrolled in a Buddhist school of meditation called Rigpa. The name has Tibetan roots, and means the knowledge that ensues from recognising one's true nature.

The meditation technique they used was to simply sit and observe the breath.

For twenty minutes.

Twice a day.

I did my best to devote myself to it. But I was pretty useless, really.

The more I tried to clear my mind, the more it filled with thoughts. The more I sat and waited for enlightenment to come, the more distracted I felt. I quickly realised that I had to change my approach to learning something new. Attempting to master meditation, assess progress, or control the experience backfired. I had to do the opposite. What I had to do, in fact, was give up. And what I had to give up was expectation. And control.

The essence of meditation is to be present, non-judgmental and heighten one's awareness. This was the opposite of my state at the time, which was either past- or future-focused, highly judgmental of any situation and of very limited awareness.

Now, after twenty-five years of pretty much daily meditation, I still consider myself a beginner. However I'm genuinely OK with that assessment. Simply accepting where I am means that something must have shifted over the years!

So even if my daily meditation consists of just a couple of minutes focusing on the breath, it is a lifeline and I feel the benefits throughout the day – which include greater presence, increased clarity and focus and more stillness.

It's the best investment I make each day.

Mindfulness is one of the most important ingredients needed to become an outstanding leader. The ability to have heightened awareness in any situation enables you to rise above your normal reactive triggers. Creating an inspired vision is nurtured by being still, focused and clear. The emotional empathy required to build great relationships is strengthened, and the art of effective decision-making is influenced by the benefits of being connected with the essence of who you are.

One of the most famous leaders of our time, who practiced daily meditation was Steve Jobs. I was blown away when I read Walter Isaacson's biography and discovered Jobs' fascination with spirituality – and in particular the influence that Zen Buddhism had on his life. According to Isaacson, Jobs believed that Zen meditation taught him to concentrate and ignore distractions. It helped him to trust his intuition and curiosity, what Buddhists call 'beginner's mind', and to pay attention in the areas of over-analysis and preconceptions. Isaacson also noted, *'Unfortunately Jobs' Zen training never quite produced in him a Zen-like calm of inner serenity and that, too, is part of his legacy.'* However, how can we know how Jobs may have been without a Zen stance!

Meditation is now on the menu at many of today's progressive organisations and educational establishments. In 2013, *Fast Company* magazine published a fascinating article entitled *Meditating Your Way To More Effective Leadership*, citing that The Drucker School of Management and Wharton Business School both offered courses in mindfulness meditation; Virginia Tech sponsors 'contemplative practices for a technological society', a conference for engineers who integrate contemplative disciplines into their work; Google offers courses in meditation, and so do companies like Aetna, Merck, General Mills – the list goes on.

These organisations are all exploring how meditation can help their leaders and employees thrive with more agility in today's fast-paced business environment. The benefits are widely publicised: sustained attention span, improved multi-tasking abilities, strengthened immune system, increased emotional intelligence and improved listening skills. There is science behind such claims. Research is fast concluding that sitting still and observing one's breath for defined periods of time is a very healthy thing to do.

One of the most helpful ways of looking at mindfuless is to consider it as less of a technique and more a way of being.

At its root, mindfulness is being awake to each moment. It encourages us to stop making assumptions based on past experience. For instance, it is very common to sit in a meeting where people are only too quick to overlay past experiences onto a scenario. These views may or may not be helpful, depending on the situation. What is more helpful is for people to be mindful of their own personal motives, possible implications of stating a point of view and taking full ownership for the impact of their contribution. It takes a split second to have this level of awareness, but it only comes through a state of mindfulness.

One of the most highly stressed people I coached was an Orthodontic dentist. Charles had a manic schedule, fitting braces day in, day out and treating around six patients at any given time as he went between his various treatment rooms. A tweak here, a fitting there, Charles's work required extreme precision both in terms of time and accuracy.

The impact of his work and accompanying stress meant that he was on the verge of total burnout. However, Charles was extremely talented which resulted in a high demand for his services. He was also passionate about the benefits of his work. Seeing people walk out of his practice with a new smile lifted his spirits. I introduced him to the idea of mindfulness.

As many do, Charles had a high initial scepticism, however he was willing to give it a go. I asked him to sit upright in his chair, rest his hands on his lap, lightly close his eyes and become aware of his breathing. I encouraged him to simply pay attention to any sensations he experienced, whether it was a restless mind or physical discomfort.

We sat together and five minutes floated by.

Then I asked Charles to gently open his eyes and recount his experience. He was surprised that even on a first attempt – although he was resistant and restless – he still had an experience of 'coming through the clouds' as he described it. I suggested that he start each and every day with this five-minute practice and notice what happened. One month later, I saw Charles again. He had managed to meditate each day and recognised that even in this short time he had developed a greater ability to observe his dental work without being so impacted by the individual needs of each patient. As Charles continued to increase his mindfulness, so did his capacity to manage his practice. The turning point came when the actual fitting of the braces became a practice of mindfulness in itself.

I believe the key to mindfulness is to keep it as simple as possible.

Here are 3 important steps to follow:

1. Set aside 5 minutes each morning. Sit upright in a chair with your hands resting lightly on your lap, palms facing upwards, eyes closed.
2. Pay attention to your breathing. Notice the quality of each inhale and exhale. There is no need to change the depth or pace of your breathing. Just observe it.

3. Allow any thoughts to be present in your consciousness. You don't have to try and stop thinking. Simply watch thoughts go by and gently bring your attention back to your breathing.

The simple ability to observe your mind sets you free.

Take a Lead

During a day, commit to having a higher level of mindfulness.

For instance, when you are facing a challenging situation before reacting in an unconscious way, let out your breath, then breathe in gently a few times, centre yourself and respond accordingly.

Don't underestimate the power of just one 5-minute meditation daily. Schedule it in.

Forgiveness is a willingness to see and do things differently

The person that suffers from holding onto resentment and grievance is you.

Chapter 40

Forgiveness Sets you Free

Liz was hailed as one of the future leaders in her organisation. Consequently, she was fast tracked for a very senior role.

In order to support this process, the company exposed her to different parts of the business and assigned her one particular role which occupied unfamiliar territory for her. As part of this assignment Liz had to report to a line manager who had an unforgiving leadership style.

Unfortunately, after only a few weeks, cracks appeared in the relationship as the line manager tried to micro-manage her. The more the manager got on Liz's case, the more antagonism ensued until the grievances took over and Liz chose to leave the company. Their plan had totally backfired.

Unfortunately, the above scenario is all too common an occurrence in organisations. As a consequence of leaders having different perspectives, unclear expectations and unresolved issues, grievances build up which can result in costly outcomes, both financial and emotional.

This doesn't have to be the case. There is a solution that tends to be overlooked and is often misperceived – the word 'forgiveness'.

Forgiveness helps you recognise the truth in any situation.

One of the greatest example of someone who applied forgiveness and through it changed the course of history, is the late Nelson Mandela. The following are two of his most poignant quotes, which I believe capture the essence of forgiveness:

'As I walked out the door toward the gate that would lead to my freedom, I knew if I didn't leave my bitterness and hatred behind, I'd still be in prison.'

And:

'You will achieve more in this world through acts of mercy than you will through acts of retribution.'

If genuinely embraced, forgiveness is the master key for restoring right perspective, clarifying misunderstandings, resolving grievances and rebuilding relationships. However, it's essential to have a thorough understanding of what forgiveness is, and the steps that go towards applying it.

We live in a world riddled with judgment and viewpoints about right and wrong. For instance, I have never met anyone who has deliberately shown up to work intending to do a bad job and underperform. However, I do see real talent written off all the time as a consequence of leaders spotting a fault and then putting someone in the 'out-box'.

When mistakes happen or conflicts arise, it is critical to ask yourself, *Am I willing to see beyond any apparent 'wrong doing' and choose to see the real issue behind the presumed issue?*

I once facilitated a session between two Executive Committees within the same globoal company. It was crucial to the success of the business that they work together; in fact their alignment would be a real competitive advantage in the industry. However, there was a long history of apparent 'wrong doings' on both sides, which would have taken an eternity to resolve. A breakthrough occurred during the meeting when one of the team members stated that the two parties should agree on a fundamental principle to guide their interactions going forward: to *'assume good intent, and that everything else would be seen as a misunderstanding'*. This sounds simple but putting it into practice was in fact an act of forgiveness. The result was a new platform to engage on, and allowed them to work together in moving forward.

It just takes one party to be willing to let go of the past, and then the other can follow.

In applying forgiveness it is important to make the distinction between an *actual* 'wrong doing', such as an illegal act versus a *perceived* 'wrong doing'. Even when a criminal act has taken place, forgiveness is possible; it does not mean the behaviour is advocated, but demonstrates a commitment to understanding the source of the issue in order to address the root cause of the behaviour.

My experience shows that behind an actual 'wrong doing' – not criminal, but serious – such as deceit, there exists a state of fear that is driving the dysfunctional behaviour. Through applying forgiveness to the situation you provide the opportunity for someone to recognise the error of their ways, take responsibility and move towards a resolution.

Forgiveness is a willingness to see things differently. Although we live in a world of multiple differences, we tend to want others to see things our way. We become attached to our point of view, often out of stubbornness, resistance or pride, which then prevents us from changing our minds. We believe that our way of seeing things is the right way. The only way. This is simply not true. There are as many ways of seeing things as there are people on this planet.

In others words, seven billion.

However, forgiveness is a commitment to going beyond what meets the naked eye and delving deeper into discovering the hidden reality – the truth.

Forgiveness requires an appetite to learn and grow.

I once coached a leader who was suddenly made redundant at the hands of a ruthless boss who had recently joined the company.

Janet was extremely popular and had enjoyed outstanding results over the years, however for some reason she just didn't fit with her new boss. As a result of the unexpected redundancy, Janet experienced a lot of initial shock and anger, but soon realised that in order to succeed in going forward with her life, she would need to seek resolution to her situation.

She chose forgiveness as the best way to move through her feelings of resentment and to gain a new perspective

How did this manifest, exactly?

Janet forgave herself for not reading the early signs her boss sent out. She forgave her manager for making her position redundant, instead of having been willing to review her role and responsibilities. She decided to take a 6-month sabbatical and use the time to focus on her own development. The irony was that 12 months later the company asked Janet to come back. They offered her a new role in a different part of the business, which she accepted. Happily.

I do believe that when you forgive you bring yourself back into alignment with a deeper truth, which then allows for the right action to occur.

Forgiveness begins and ends with ourselves.

When we think of forgiveness, we tend to hold it as an act we do for others. It's not. We do it for ourselves. When we hold onto grievances, upsets and resentments the only person we hurt is us. To quote Nelson Mandela again, *'Resentment is like drinking poison and then hoping it will kill your enemies.'*

When we refuse to forgive, others move forward with their lives, but we are trapped by our own grievances. A grievance is simply a form of self-attack which limits us from examining the truth about ourselves.

Take Sam. A high-flying lawyer with a lot of resentment about being in the legal profession. Sam held his father accountable for having pushed him in the direction of law, he felt resentful and so refused to have a relationship with him. Able to avoid his father as an adult, it became more difficult when he started his own family as Sam had enjoyed a great relationship with his grandfather, and wanted the same thing for his children with their grandfather. This meant resolving his relationship with his dad.

Like Janet, Sam chose to put forgiveness at the top of his coaching agenda. It wasn't an easy choice, but he wanted to see how it would pan out.

One of the tools I use to facilitate the process of forgiveness is through letter writing. This is an extremely powerful way of articulating thoughts and feelings without having direct confrontation. I took Sam through the steps, suggesting he write a letter to his father following 3 different formats:

1. A Grievance Letter

The purpose of a grievance letter is just that – to air your grievances, giving you the chance to articulate unresolved thoughts and to express feelings of resentment in order to see exactly how you are feeling. In this letter, Sam wrote down all his judgments of his father, recounting how his father relentlessly pushed him to study hour after hour, without any appreciation of the destructive impact that it had on him. Sam wrote down how he blamed his father for forcing him into Law and failing to understand his true passions and desires.

2. A Responsibility Letter

The purpose of a responsibility letter is to take full ownership of the experience that you had in the past with the person you are writing to, and to remove all blame from them. This is a very tough letter to write because the ego will resist, will want to pin blame on the other and avoid taking responsibility for your own experience.

So in this version Sam wrote, *My feelings of resentment for you (his father) spring from my own failure to stand up for myself and to choose a career in another profession. I did not know myself well enough. I was not able to articulate what I really wanted. I know that you were driven by your own father to succeed as a lawyer, and I imagine that your own personal dilemma with the law profession got projected on to me.* In truth Sam saw that he was not a victim of his father, and could make other choices if he wanted to.

3. A Forgiveness Letter

The purpose of this letter is to be honest about how you feel, to take responsibility for your own experience and to move towards a place of resolution. In his final letter, Sam was able to write down the facts of the situation as he saw them, explain his feelings, recognise any projection that he had placed on his father, and forgive his father for the perceived misunderstanding.

He wrote: *I appreciate how difficult it must have been for you with your own father breathing down your neck to be successful as a lawyer. I was also unable to understand the pressures of providing for a family until I got there myself. Now I can see why you were so determined for me to succeed as a lawyer. You wanted the best for me, but were limited in your own perspective about what that could look like. Although I have wrestled with being a lawyer, I am grateful for the training it has given me and forgive you for pushing me against my will.*

Sam recognised that his father had done the best he could with the limited awareness he had and that continuing to hold grievances against him was a futile exercise.

These letters are for your own use. You certainly don't send the first two. You might send the third version if you have genuinely moved to a place of forgiveness. The way to test if this has occurred is that when you hold the person in your mind's eye, you feel a sense of peace and non-judgment. If, on the other hand, you notice yourself still feeling angry or resentful, then you are still secretly holding onto a grievance and your forgiveness is not yet complete.

Don't give up. Forgiveness sets you free.

One of the greatest benefits of forgiveness is that it liberates you from your own self-attacks. Most leaders I know are far more critical of themselves than of others. In fact, if they talked to others in the way they talked to themselves they wouldn't have many followers! Constant self-criticism undermines your sense of value and worth. As you give up self-attack you discover a new freedom to speak up, express yourself and be fully authentic.

Forgiveness also brings you peace of mind. Probably one of the main qualities lacking in leaders I coach is an experience of genuine peace. The restless pursuit of excellence often interferes with the ability to access the quiet mind, which is always present underneath the daily turbulence. Forgiveness takes you back to a sense of peace, reminding you of what is real and most important. For example, if you're struggling in a relationship – whether it's with a colleague, customer, investor or supplier, forgiveness will elevate your thinking so that you go beyond surface issues and approach the relationship from a peaceful base.

The key to forgiveness is willingness. Forgiveness has its own intelligence. As you make yourself available to forgive, it will show you the way. Set your intent to forgive, and see yourself as a forgiving person. Forgiveness is not a sign of weakness. Clearly, one of the greatest strengths in a leader is the ability to see things differently in order to discover the truth. I would like to leave the last word on forgiveness, once again, to Nelson Mandela:

> *'What counts in life is not the mere*
> *fact that we have lived.*
> *It is what difference we have made*
> *to the lives of others that will determine*
> *the significance of the life we lead.'*

Take a Lead

Think of a relationship where you hold a grievance. Set aside 60 minutes to write initial versions of the 3 types of letter:

Grievance letter

Responsibility letter

Forgiveness letter

Notice how you feel once completed. Now, recall this person. If there are still unresolved feelings present, be prepared to keep writing different versions of the letter until genuine forgiveness has taken place and you are at peace.

Commit to learning about forgiveness so that you develop a deep understanding of what it is, and be willing to apply it every day.

What is love?

Love is more than an emotion. It is a way of being.

Chapter 41

Lead with Love

In the past, the idea of even mentioning love in the workplace would have been unthinkable. Yet one of the biggest shifts I have witnessed over the last few years is the concept of love taking much more of a centre stage.

Now, companies and brands are putting 'love' at the heart of their identity. This means that as a leader you need to work out what love means to you and how to lead with love.

These three paradigms can help to explore what love means from the leadership perspective:

1) Love as a verb: what we *do*.
2) Love as an emotion: how we *feel*.
3) Love as a mindset: who we *are*.

1) Love as a verb

Steve Jobs' remarkable commencement address to students at Stanford in 2005 captures the essence of love as a verb:

'Sometimes life is going to hit you in the head with a brick. Don't lose faith. I'm convinced that the only thing that kept me going was that I loved what I did. You've got to find

what you love. Your work is going to fill a large part of your life, and the only way to be truly satisfied is to do what you believe is great work; and the only way to do great work is to love what you do. If you haven't found it yet keep looking, and don't settle. As with all matters of the heart you'll know when you find it. And like with any great relationship it just gets better and better as the years roll on.'

Loving what you do is one of the most critical aspects of leadership. If you don't love what you do there is no way that you will be able to inspire and engage others, stay energised and passionate, be creative and innovative and make a meaningful difference.

It is essential to figure out what you love to do. Loving what you do means doing what turns you on. Discovering your real passion. Following your obsession. Letting the love of what you do take you over.

Lawrence was on the succession ladder to take up a position of leadership. But could he actually step up as a leader? He was brilliant in his speciality area, however his company's main concern about him taking on a wider leadership role was his visible lack of passion. In particular, the Executive Committee could not see whether he loved what he did enough to move on to the next phase. It was a very interesting case because Lawrence was extremely capable, and had a very high IQ, but his apparent lack of loving what he did was the stumbling block. As part of my coaching programme with him, I presented Lawrence with this information in the form of a 360-feedback process.

The results did not surprise him.

What transpired when we discussed the feedback findings was that Lawrence loved the technical aspect of his role, which he was able to practice in relative isolation.

He was not sure if he wanted to take on the very different requirements of a leadership role, and so his ambivalence towards leadership came through.

I have found this to be a common dilemma in developing leaders in large organisations.

An individual is recruited because they show great ability and clearly love what they do. An ensuing promotion brings new responsibilities, which they might not love as much – such as managing large numbers of people on a daily basis.

These new roles can bring up feelings of resentment alongside the happiness and pride that they also evoke, challenging an employee with the wider demands being placed on them, and seemingly taking them away from what they love and are good at. It requires a high dosage of self-awareness and honesty to reconcile the two and make the right choice. You may choose to stay a technical expert, or expand your abilities and learn to love what leadership entails.

Jake is one of the former.

He is one of the most inspirational leaders I know, and loves what he does. Probably the most successful general manager in his company, Jake is very clear that his love lies in running a single operation, which gives him the opportunity to put his ideas into action and create a unique experience for his customers. The corporate side of the company is forever knocking on his door trying to entice him to take on a wider role. Every time it comes around Jake refuses an upward move. He knows very well that sitting in a glass office would take him away from the three things he most loves – growing a brilliant team; engaging with customers at the front line; and being able to implement innovative ideas quickly.

How do you know whether you love what you do?

You never clock watch.
You don't question your commitment.
You care deeply about the end result.
Your intrinsic motivation drives you.

Think of Richard Branson, whom I've mentioned before and whose love of listening to music with friends was the catalyst for Virgin Records. And Bill Gates, whose love of empowering people with knowledge through easy-to-use software inspired Microsoft. Or Oprah Winfrey, whose love of helping others live their best lives touches her millions of viewers daily.

2) Love as an emotion

The field of EQ – Emotional Intelligence – finally legitimised the importance of working with feelings. Given the power of emotion it was crazy that it hadn't come into play before and not to have acknowledged the pivotal role emotion in the way people work together – its ability to help or hinder success. There is no emotion more impactful than love.

According to the online music research project, *allmusic*, there have been 1028 individual songs released to date with the word 'love' in the title. And that's not including those with 'love' in the song itself. At the end of the day what people want is to love and be loved, whether they talk about it as feeling valued, being respected and trusted, or gaining recognition.

In the workplace the closest companies get to measuring love – which I'd break down into passion, talent, dedication, performance, fulfillment – is through their employee engagement. The world's top-performing organisations understand that love is the most powerful driving force that determines top notch performance. At the heart of this engagement is:

- feeling proud to work for that specific company
- being happy to come into work
- advocating the company to others
- putting in discretionary effort
- gaining a sense of achievement from the job

Gallup, one of today's leading research companies on human nature and behaviour, shows that approximately 50% of employees are actively disengaged. These are people who do not feel valued at work.

Half the workforce.

That's a big number and it has a profound ripple effect – in both damaging the spirits of people around them as well as eroding a company's bottom line. In the US, Gallup estimates this cost to the bottom line as being over $300 billion in lost productivity alone. In contrast, high performing organisations show an engagement ratio of more than 9:1.

So how does a leader create an environment in which people feel a real love for what they do?

First, by showing it themselves.

Jessica is the kind of leader who people feel genuine love for. I had the joy of coaching her team, and on the last round of interviews I conducted her team members came up with comments like:

- She has a transparent way of working, which people love.
- She has amazing intuition about different personalities, which is impressive.
- She is very fair in her treatment of people.
- She gives tough love when required, lets people get on with their job and provides great advice when relevant.

In order for people to feel love for your way, you must show you care passionately about all aspects of leadership.

You must stand for something that inspires, whether it's building great brands, creating unbeatable customer experience or developing an inspiring workplace.

One leader I worked with stood for three things – people, service and profit. His mantra to his leadership team was that he was committed to helping them realise their dreams, and wanted to make each of them a millionaire. This was his pledge. Whether you agree with it or not, his team loved him: they knew what he cared about them, and he delivered on his promises.

On the other hand, I once found myself in a company where the credibility of the CEO got blown out of the water because although he *talked* about valuing his people, he allowed his Executive Committee to treat employees in an underhand way and failed to address this type of behaviour. You need to show how much you care, and let people feel it, rather than simply paying lip service.

3) Love as a mindset

The third paradigm is that love is part of the identity you create, as a result of the mindset you adopt.

Consider the idea that love is the essence of you. It is the authentic you. Seeing yourself as committed to love makes it a natural state. I know that may appear a radical concept. However, taking a lead demands that we stretch ourselves in new ways. Having a 'love mindset' means the following:

- Showing genuine care and compassion
- Putting forgiveness into action
- Having a non-judgmental attitude
- Looking for, and focusing on, the best in people
- Respecting and trusting others
- Having open and honest conversations

- Being prepared to overcome all difficulties by making love more important than anything else

Leaders who have this mindset take a stand for creating environments where people can flourish. They commit to removing interferences so that others can be their real selves. They do not collude with organisation politics, which can so often distract or damage people and their performance. A leader committed to love is prepared to have the difficult conversations most people avoid. They have the ability to give honest feedback, as they come from a truly genuine loving place. Being a leader with love at your core does not mean that you talk about love. Your actions become far more meaningful and powerful for others, as they experience a sense of safety because of your loving presence in a fear-based world.

Love is not something you have to do, earn or achieve. It is a state of mind and a way of being. Love inspires greatness. Love encourages growth. Love builds relationships. Love nurtures creativity.

In fact, there is no problem that love cannot help overcome.

Take a Lead

Define your philosophy about love.

Reflect upon the 3 paradigms of love – verb, emotion, mindset – to discover what love means to you and how you can lead with love.

Our instinct to grow is one of the most basic needs we must meet in order to flourish

Great leaders put their own personal growth at the heart of their leadership.

Chapter 42

Keep Growing

I maintain that the most fundamental aspect to being a great leader is an enduring commitment to continual personal growth.

The trouble is that once people get into positions of leadership they have a tendency to take their eye off their own growth.

Take Marianne, for example. She had applied herself diligently on her way up the leadership ladder. As is the case with many promotions, her success was primarily as a result of her functional capability. Faced with the opportunity to lead a large division, Marianne recognised that in order to succeed she needed to grow. Thankfully she had a very supportive boss who fully understood her dilemma and encouraged Marianne to get the help required to accelerate her growth. As part of her promotion, Marianne attended an assessment center in order to create a clear picture of her strengths and development opportunities.

The assessment covered three main areas:

- Cognitive agility
- Commercial agility
- Learning agility

As is the case with many senior executives, Marianne scored highly on the first two agilities, which are mainly IQ-based. However, learning agility is much more closely linked to EQ. That's when I was called in.

We sat down together in her top floor office to analyse the results. What became very clear was that in order to grow Marianne needed to focus on a few key themes:

- Developing visionary leadership
- Communicating a compelling picture to her team
- Inspiring her team to grow

I could tell this would be a big stretch for Marianne, as she had never consciously applied herself to these qualities. In order to ensure that she was fully on board, we started off by focusing on any sub-conscious resistance Marianne might have to growing. Unless you face any resistance up front, it can sabotage growth going forward.

Marianne came up with several key factors that could get in the way. Take a look at these thoughts and see if they ring any bells:

- *Investing time in my growth will distract me from delivering results.*
- *I might not like who I turn into because it won't be the real me.*
- *I don't want to have to dredge up the past in order to grow into the future.*
- *It's a sign of weakness having to admit you need to grow.*

Putting these concerns on the table allowed Marianne to step back and look at them rationally in the cool light of day. As I challenged her on the truth of these concerns, she saw they were not logical and was able to conclude the following:

- *Investing time in my growth will be a key enabler for delivering results.*
- *If I don't grow then my team won't grow and if the team doesn't grow the business can't grow.*
- *In the absence of growth I could end up doing the same old stuff I've done before, which will not help me succeed going forward.*
- *Focusing on my growth will actually help me become more of the real me. Unless I challenge myself to grow I won't fulfill my potential.*
- *Applying myself to my growth is a future-orientated activity. There is no need to go back into the past in order to create the future I want.*
- *It's a sign of my strength and humility to recognise and admit that I need to grow.*

On the back of this new insight Marianne was able to put together a robust personal development plan to guide her growth. She found it extremely energising and was given fresh focus and a solid perspective for overcoming the challenges ahead.

One of the biggest failings you face is to not see your own blind spots. It can be obvious to others what you need to do differently to grow, but if you're not prepared to take ownership of your growth agenda – and let others know you're on the case – then it could even mean your downfall.

I believe that our instinct to grow is one of the most basic needs we must meet in order to flourish.

So how come we so quickly lose our innate hunger and desire for growth?

Speaking for myself, it was the formal education I received at school. We assume the purpose of school is to nurture our growth, however it often has the opposite effect and instead of opening the appetite for learning, shuts it down. The learning styles and subjects I was exposed to did not work for me at all, in fact they switched me off. It was only when I discovered the world of personal development that my passion for real growth was ignited. I was suddenly genuinely interested in a subject, and found that I had an insatiable appetite – I couldn't lay my hands on enough information, or experience enough of this new world. My learning curve accelerated, I felt inspired, I became challenged, and what I learnt is that when we are truly interested in something – and it's shared with us in a way that we relate to – we instinctively want to grow.

This is very apparent to me as a parent. As I write this book, I watch my daughter studying for her 11+ exams. I see how she truly engages when her learning is dynamic and fun, and is able to apply a range of learning styles – kinesthetic, auditory and visual. However it is still a real challenge when activities with friends is so much more appealing. Active parenting is really no different to being a leader. Meeting the challenge of inspiring your children is a commitment to your own continual growth. I find that the most effective way of doing this is to be an example, so I undertook to walk the path with her through her numeracy and literature topics. It wasn't as bad the second time around!

The leaders I admire most have all put personal growth at the top of their agendas. One leader encourages his people to ring-fence 10% of their time in order to focus on their own personal development. This equates to approximately five hours of their working week where they have permission to take the time to read, reflect, study, get coached, attend training, try a new discipline at work – anything that helps them consciously grow.

By deliberately encouraging your own growth you will reap the rewards of lifelong learning.

The day you stop growing is the day you stop leading.

Take a Lead

Decide how you want to grow.

Reflect upon the development theme that will make the biggest difference to your leadership effectiveness and make your growth a priority.

Make wisdom your learning curve

What defines you as a leader is knowing the right thing to do, and acting on that knowledge.

Chapter 43

Unlocking Wisdom

I used to suffer from the feeling that other people knew better.

About pretty much everything.

Consequently, I would follow other people's perspectives, take on their ideas or ways of seeing the world, while relegating my own internal wisdom to a quiet whisper.

For example, I remained at music school when I would have rather left to follow my passion for the sporting world; I allowed an editor to convince me about a book title which I didn't believe was the right one; and I often played second fiddle to business partners, failing to put across my own valid points of view.

Things continued along this vein until I was introduced to the Enneagram system and was able to both define and address my personality type (see Chapter 8). I suddenly saw, in a very practical way, that the majority of the conflict I had experienced was due to not trusting my own, inner wisdom.

There are not many things that I am absolute about, but one thing I know is that everyone has their own inner wisdom. I believe that a genuine act of leadership is to be able to access that wisdom, listen to it and act upon the guidance you discover.

When I challenge most leaders with the idea that they are wise they often refute it. This is usually because the concept of wisdom is misunderstood. The ego tends to define wisdom as a competitive state. For instance, people assuming they know better and being inflexible as to others' perspective.

When people behave from these positions the outcome is one of conflict and disengagement.

The wisdom I am referring to is rather an innate knowing – what you know instinctively.

Real wisdom contains an infectious energy: it brings people together, unleashes creativity, stimulates ideas and results in a sense of harmony. All the major decisions that I have made in my life have been born out of this real wisdom which has over-ridden all real confusion. Even though I didn't know what would be on the other side when I quit the music world, I was driven by a sense of inner knowing that I had to do it; signing my first book contract was a real leap of faith as I only had a book outline as my guide; getting married took me way beyond what I thought I was able to commit to in a relationship; and having kids stretched me right past my rational mind most of the time! Even now, carrying out my work commitments takes me over what I logically think is possible, resulting in levels of fulfillment I still find hard to believe.

Consider this: You are a wise human being. You have innate wisdom that simply exists. Part of your responsibility as a leader is to realise your own wisdom and follow it.

I love the idea of following one's wisdom. The great philosopher Joseph Campbell talked about 'Following your bliss.' I would go further, and say that by following your wisdom you will find your bliss.

One of the biggest challenges in our information-based world is that there is so much at our fingertips. We have pieces of 'wisdom' coming at us from all sides, and through it we gain more and more knowledge. However, there is a big difference between information, or even knowledge, and wisdom. While there is no doubt that it is extremely useful to know what is going on in the world – whether it be the news, business issues, economics, politics, art, science, cultures, religions or any other number of fascinating topics that we are blessed to be able to Google – it can never replace real wisdom, and the fact that it is ours by birthright.

Real wisdom comes through stillness and contemplation.

The art is to identify that particular voice in your being that is your voice of true inner wisdom. It can be like a child nudging you until you stop and give it attention, or a deep thirst that is not satisfied until you've had a good long drink. It's helpful to recognise how you access your wisdom. Some people are more auditory, and 'hear' their wisdom through words. Others are more visual and 'see' images or pictures that allow their wisdom to shine through. Then there are those who are more kinesthetic and 'feel' their wisdom coming through via their emotional state. It doesn't matter how you access it, the important thing is that you create sufficient time and space to discover it.

I find one of the most effective ways of getting in touch with my wisdom is by writing freestyle. Basically, the act of writing is really an act of listening. Writing allows you to access your inner voice, to clarify what is present for you and to help you to distinguish between what is meaningful and what is trivial.

I once coached an entrepreneur – a brilliant creative, who ran her own successful business, supported her husband's career, took pleasure in mothering her gorgeous kids and had created a beautiful home. Amanda was by anyone's standards a highly capable leader and yet she was plagued by self-doubt. It limited her effectiveness and diminished her fulfillment. I confronted her with the idea that she had real wisdom, and could access it, however she felt extremely uncomfortable at the thought of listening to and acting upon her wisdom in a conscious way.

I tasked her with keeping a 'wisdom journal' in which she could write down daily thoughts. At first she actively resisted the idea and found any excuse not to spend even 5 minutes a day on it. So I asked her to suspend judgment and simply to treat it as a small experiment to see if she noticed any responses to questions like, What did I learn today? What was the wisest decision I made today? What decision do I know I should have made, but didn't? If I could access my inner wisdom what would I have done differently today?

Taking small steps, Amanda opened up to the idea that she might have an inner wisdom that could help her outer life. I invited her to see wisdom as her learning curve. I told her that if she was genuinely committed to discovering her wisdom there would be a discipline involved, such as committing to her writing. After her initial resistance, she became a willing student and over time developed an ability to really find wisdom in her journal. Her writing became a daily habit, and her journal a friend that enabled her to become more tuned in to what was really going on in her mind. As she became adept at expressing her wisdom, the benefits trickled into her world. For instance, she came to realise that she needed a different type of support team around her, so began redefining the roles in her company and recruiting the kind of people that would allow her own talent and energy the freedom and expression needed.

Though there were difficult conversations she needed to have, she managed to let go those people that drained her.

She felt more at peace with her life choices than she ever had before, and actively spent her time with those who enriched her.

A true leader allows their innate wisdom to guide and inspire both their decisions and actions.

Take a Lead

Keep a wisdom journal.

On a daily basis use some wisdom-based questions to stimulate your reflections, e.g. upon awakening ask yourself:

• *How will I know at the end of the day if I've been wise or not?*

If you have a specific challenge in a day write down:

• *What would my wisdom have me think, say, or do in this situation?*

At the end of a day make a note of the following:

• *What is the wisest thing I accomplished today?*

What's your style?

Each great leader has several ways of leading,

it's inherent in our DNA.

Chapter 44

Leadership Styles

Ever heard of the pioneering work of Daniel Goleman?

He popularised the concept of Emotional Intelligence, and is a man I have enormous respect for.

His article, *Leadership That Gets Results* (*Harvard Business Review*, March 2000) is a brilliant portrayal of six different leadership styles, each of which has a particular impact on the culture of any particular organisation. Goleman writes about the styles as if they were different golf clubs, and the same way any good golfer knows which club to use depending on the hole he's facing, a great leader knows which style to bring out for each situation.

Goleman's research outlines the following predominant styles for effective leadership:

Authoritative
Coercive
Pace-setting
Democratic
Affiliative
Coaching

He believes that great leaders need to demonstrate at least 3-4 of these styles fluently.

What I find fascinating is how each style affects an organisational climate – including behavioural traits like flexibility, responsibility, standards, rewards, clarity and commitment. Goleman's study shows that the most positive style to use over time is *authoritative*, which brings people together, focusing on a common goal; and the most negative one is *pace-setting*, where a leader will set such high standards for performance that his or her drive for results leaves people disengaged or burnt out.

What is your preferred style of leadership? What style of leadership would your people say you exhibit?

These are the two initial questions I put forward to leaders on my leadership development programmes. Once I have their own self-assessment, I then go back to their team members to ask what style of leadership they demonstrate. It's very revealing.

On one programme, a leader who had a very high emotional intelligence was able to accurately describe his leadership style. Greg had an approach based on 'freedom within a framework'. It meant that he liked to be highly directive until the moment he saw there was sufficient movement in the direction he wanted, at which point he would ease off. Greg's people used the exact same phrase to explain his style. However, they also said that while his approach worked very well initially – especially when the company was going through considerable change and therefore needed high levels of direction – over time it resulted in lower engagement levels, as it detracted from people's initiative and ownership of the direction headed in.

Greg paid attention to this, and as a result of his heightened awareness saw that he needed to broaden his style and put far more emphasis on *authoritative, democratic* and *coaching* styles in order to really take his people with him.

Highly respectful of Goleman's work, I have identified five styles that my own work has uncovered, which I encourage leaders to build into their repertoire. They are:

Visionary
Collaborative
Directive
Enabling
Driven

1. Visionary Style

Leaders may initially feel less comfortable with a visionary style. However, while developing this quality does not mean becoming a Steve Jobs or Richard Branson, it does require having a 'growth mindset' where you become willing to explore new ideas, possibilities are generated that will stretch you, and you are challenged to do things differently. A visionary style demands that you set aside time to reflect on the big picture and ask some important questions. *Where am I now? What direction do I want to go? What will it take to get there?* Any leader can become more visionary with the right motivation and willingness to think ahead.

Take Lucy, who had a background in marketing and finance when she secured her role as CEO for a large multinational. This particular company had reached a point in its evolution where it was being run by a set of numbers, but lacked true inspiration and clear direction. This played to Lucy's strengths. Her high financial literacy meant that she could relate to the finance department that dominated the running of the company. However, what was required to take the company into the future was a more compelling vision to inspire and engage people, in order for it to become truly great.

Lucy brought together her top 100 senior leaders for a three-day retreat, focusing on creating a shared vision in a collaborative way. This idea was met with some initial resistance, however she was able to present a very clear case for the change required in the company, which influenced people to look at things differently. Together, the top leaders defined their vision for the next five years and showed a complete commitment to engaging the rest of the organisation with their renewed focus.

2. Collaborative Style

This can be one of the most misunderstood approaches in leadership. While I appreciate that in large, global matrix-structured companies it is challenging to collaborate in an effective way, all too often it's used a reason for not getting a job done. A good collaborative leader recognises that the way to create sustainable success is to be inclusive; to involve others in decision-making processes and to invest in engaging people through clear communication. A collaborative leader knows that it's essential to be able to make the tough calls when required to, and ensures that collaboration is never used as an excuse to delay progress.

Martin was exemplary at demonstrating a collaborative style, and I had the privilege of coaching his leadership team on their journey to deliver the largest construction programme in Europe at that time. How did he do it? Although there was an almost overwhelming agenda, Martin spent a lot of time up front, ensuring that everyone had sufficient input into all stages of putting their plan into place.

On our first offsite meeting together, we defined the exact success criteria for the team and agreed as to how they would work together in order to deliver. Some team members were frustrated by the apparent lack of progress through being collaborative, however over the following 18-months of consistently engaging people through seeking their opinion, tweaking all elements of the operation to reflect different points of view and adapting his own leadership style when required, Martin built one of the most high performing and collaborative teams I have witnessed.

As you develop a greater collaborative style it's important to contextualise it within your vision so that people can really understand where you are coming from. A collaborative style can appear vague or even weak unless it's accompanied by a strong dose of vision, which inspires people to recognise the massive value of working closely together.

3. Directive Style

If a fire alarm went off right now and I started asking how you felt or what you were thinking, you certainly wouldn't rate me as an effective leader! In any crisis, a directive style is necessary to give others the clarity they need to move forward. I saw this style used to great effect during the economic crisis of 2008 when organisations required strong and decisive leadership to keep them afloat. A directive style was the right approach when a global bank went public with their new company purpose, values and behaviours and demonstrated a non-compromising approach as they set expectations with their global workforce as to how they would integrate their new way of working going forward.

Some leaders ironically feel uncomfortable at being directive, as they don't like telling people what to do. This is a limited view. The true definition of a directive style is the willingness to take a stand about what's most important and to provide clear direction. This approach gives others a solid starting point, allowing others to identify whether this is the right option to take – and if it is combined with collaboration, it means that you can then work together to agree on the best solutions. It's essential to be very clear about a true directive style and any form of bullying or fear tactic, as any behaviour that results in others feeling humiliated, scared, put down or compromised is inappropriate and unacceptable. I recognise that this kind of behaviour is still to be found even in the most enlightened organisations, but I'm glad to report that I see more and more leaders moving quickly to stamp it out.

4. Enabling Style

One of the main misperceptions of demonstrating an enabling style is time. Leaders tend to think that they don't have enough time to develop others. My view is that they don't have enough time not to!

If you are not focused on encouraging your people to perform at their best at all times, then you will be in trouble. Any leadership agenda today is far too large and complex for one individual to deliver independently. The only way leaders can succeed is through nurturing the ability of their people. A leader using the enabling style will see different situations as opportunities to encourage others to think more clearly, trust their own judgment, take initiative and be more collaborative. This could take the form of a corridor conversation, a meeting, e-mail or a formal one-to-one. In other words there are multiple ways to enable others. But it does require a genuine commitment to help people fulfill their potential. An enabling leader will put coaching, mentoring and facilitation at the heart of their leadership and commit to creating an environment in which others can be the best versions of themselves.

5. Driven Style

Leadership is about getting results and driving performance. While it matters how visionary, collaborative, directive and enabling you are as a leader, unless you achieve tangible results, your leadership will be threatened. Your credibility lies in your results and your reputation is enhanced by delivering on your promises.

Jane was a leader whose high drive for results combined with the four other styles, enabled her to rise quickly through her organisation until she reached the heights of heading up a large division. The timing was fortunate in that the need in the division at her point of entry was performance-focused. Her predecessor had worked hard at creating a vision for the division through using a collaborative and enabling style. Now was the time to put a relentless focus on execution in order to help grow the company and build a solid reputation in the marketplace.

Jane made it very clear to her team what results she expected from them. Each target was clearly articulated with a plan to support delivery. Every meeting focused heavily on tracking progress and having the tough conversations needed to accelerate results. Her leadership team was energised by this approach. It unlocked their passion for achieving great things and together they outperformed market expectations and their internal targets. Thankfully Jane was very mindful of the impact of a driven style over time. As soon as momentum had been established, she ensured that her people had the right support to deliver, and the space to breathe so that they could stay on top of their game.

My personal preference is to be both highly collaborative and enabling. I'm a team player and find my greatest reward in helping others fulfill their potential. As a consequence I've had to focus very hard on developing my ability to become more visionary, rather than relying on others to see the big picture. I've also had to strengthen my backbone to become more directive when required. I took it as a compliment recently when I got feedback from a client saying that I was being overly instructive and should demonstrate more of an open approach. It showed me that I had now developed the ability to be clearer and firmer and had managed to incorporate greater breadth in my style.

Real leadership is both a skill and an art: becoming highly attuned and able to adapt your style according to the situation you face is the former; doing it fluently and effortlessly the latter, and comes about as a result of heightened awareness and practice. *I encourage you to master both.*

The choice of leadership style is yours.

Take a Lead

On a scale of 1-5 (1 = very low, 5 = very high) rate your preference against the 5 leadership styles:

1. Visionary

2. Collaborative

3. Enabling

4. Directive

5. Driven

Reflect upon the situations that you face and consider what styles are appropriate to demonstrate. Commit to flexing your style accordingly in order to become the best leader you can be.

Trust is everything

No trust? No leadership.

Chapter 45

Deepen Trust

Everywhere I work, I see *one* underlying message highlighted time and time again – by individuals, teams and organisations as a fundamental requirement for success. That message is trust.

Trust is the glue that binds relationships together.

It is the criteria by which people measure whether they can do business together. The way by which brands build customer love. In the absence of trust, suspicions run high, misunderstandings rule and loyalty is thin on the ground.

I believe that the majority of people are willing to trust, however as soon as there is any perceived evidence as a reason not to, then it is quickly lost.

I once supported a leadership team struggling to manage one of their most valuable customer relationships. Historically, the relationship had been adversarial in nature, and as a member of the customer group described it, 'A day without a fight was perceived as a wasted day.' Engaging with both sides I quickly saw that each clearly recognised the potential of working together in true partnership, and saw that it would be a competitive advantage in their industry.

However, they also knew that a deep trust had to be built in order to enable the right level of alignment.

An initial meeting was set up with the primary purpose of building trust.

The meeting began by focusing on a well-informed agenda: laying out the background and context of the partnership, seeing the big picture of a future direction and clarifying the commercial reason for focusing on shared priorities. But there was still a strong amount of resistance to gaining real alignment.

The turning point came with trying to move forward in a different way, addressing barriers head on. Suddenly what came to light was the customer's belief that my client's primary interest was their own gain – even at the latter's expense. A brave admission. Acknowledgement from the other party – an equally brave admission – enabled small steps to be taken in laying a foundation of trust for the future. It was a slow journey, and took the best part of 18 months to reach a point where trust eventually led the partnership – but it was accomplished.

If you are being objective, do you know how people would rate the degree of trust you elicit as a leader? If trust is a key differentiator between good and great relationships, how do you deliberately develop trust?

Trust is the currency of my work. Unless individuals trust me it's not going to be possible to have a coaching relationship. Unless teams trust me we cannot work together. Unless organisations trust me, I will not be able to develop their senior leaders. Ahead of starting any coaching relationship I set up a 'chemistry' meeting, the purpose of which is to test if there is the sufficient basis for trust to develop. I make an agreement with any team leader I work with that if one member of the team vetoes my involvement then we will not continue, as the trust will be compromised. I deliberately challenge trust levels every step of the way in my client relationships so that nothing gets taken for granted. As a consequence, the feedback I mostly receive is that trust runs high, due to my open approach and willingness to develop trust on a consistent basis.

But what is trust, exactly?

I have found five key steps for developing and deepening it:

First, resolve any personal issues of mistrust

At the age of 16, following the breakdown of my parents' marriage, my levels of trust dropped to an all-time low. Up until then I had taken certain things for granted in life. However the realisation that their marriage was over swept away all my points of stability and I became highly untrusting of others. I became increasingly independent, and refused to let anyone get too close to me in case I got knocked again. In fact my biggest barrier to progressing in my relationship with my wife, was to not trust the love she extended to me. Thankfully, she did not give up and over time our ability to work through any issue that surfaced enabled me to trust again.

- *What unresolved issues do you have that block your trust?*
- *Are they connected with personal or professional relationships?*
- *Do they have their roots in your perception of the world?*
- *Do you have concerns about money, work, politics, religion, businesses, or any other factors that cause you to have low trust levels?*

Your ability to deepen trust levels will result in having a clearer perspective about trust in the world.

Second, seek feedback as to how trustworthy you come across

If you genuinely believe that you demonstrate trust in your relationships, then it should be a non-issue to ask for candid feedback about how you really do come across. When I first met Allie she was smiling and exuded confidence. She told me that she prided herself on the extent of trust she built in relationships, and that transparency was her middle name. However, what revealed itself was something quite different. As Allie progressed upwards in her organisation she became more thinly spread, and after 18 months I carried out a 360-feedback exercise. To Allie's great surprise, comments came back questioning her sincerity. The view was that she would tell people what she thought they wanted to hear, thus planting a seed of doubt as to her true motives and, ultimately, trustworthiness.

Getting this feedback challenged Allie's understanding of herself and personal integrity to the core. As we worked through the findings she saw that unless people knew her well, they would define her desire to empathise with others as chameleon-like behaviour. Allie swallowed the bitter pill, took the message on board and from then on gave clear signals as to where she was coming from in order to close any gap in perception about her levels of real care and trustworthiness.

Third, be fact-based in your decision making

I was sitting in an executive committee meeting, listening to a conversation about a company's future growth. Attention was focused on one business unit in particular. Quick remarks were being fired off as to how the unit should be closed down, as it appeared to no longer fit in with future plans. But according to whom and what? When the CEO began to challenge the 'facts', no one could back up their claims with any real evidence-based findings to give an informed reason. Organisational myths had arisen regarding the unit which could not be substantiated, and it had come close to grave jeopardy for nothing.

Unfortunately, this happens all too frequently, as leaders working at high speed and under large amounts of pressure become only too happy to take comments at face value, which can have serious implications for individuals, teams and the company itself if acted upon. Your willingness to adopt a fact-based approach will deepen trust. It will indicate that you have an open mind, are a keen listener and are committed to doing the right thing even if it takes more time and effort.

Fourth, make transparency your signature

The huge impact of a leader's openness and honesty never ceases to amaze me. I found myself facilitating a senior leadership meeting for a team that had some serious under-performance issues in their business. They had recently been subjected to a review process, which resulted in a very tight programme plan being implemented that was specifically designed to help turn the business around. Although this provided a lot of clarity about what they would focus on delivering together, it had not addressed the wider issues of how they would behave together.

Henry, the leader of the team, although new to the top job, was seasoned in the company and well-known to each member of the team. At the outset of this introductory workshop one of his team members had the courage to say that the success of the turnaround would be largely dependent on Henry being able to role model the behaviours that were needed. Henry responded superbly. He candidly spoke up about the need to do things differently and his desire to develop a personal signature with transparency at the heart of it. Many of the problematic issues had resulted from a lack of openness and honesty with employees, customers and shareholders and now it was time to turn things around. I could feel the mix of relief and subsequent anticipation as Henry seized the challenge.

How transparent are you in the way you lead? Do you openly share with others your hopes, concerns, strengths and development areas? There is a direct correlation between transparency and trust, and the way to build the latter is to embrace the former.

Last, give trust to gain it

My first step in working with a team is to interview each member about the current effectiveness of the team and its leader. On one occasion, I was warned about a team member who had a highly confrontational style. Sure enough, even before I had introduced myself Lawrence started grilling me about my credentials and why I was even working with the team. A large man, he had no qualms about his confrontational stance. Instead of going through my usual interviewing questions, I went straight for the section about his own team leader. His response to my question: *What do you value about your team leader?* triggered the reaction: *I don't value him because I don't trust him.* When I probed further, he went on to disclose that his starting point in any new relationship was to withold trust until they had proved their reliability.

Later, when I sat down with Ted, his team leader, in order to debrief him on the findings, he related immediately, and pointed out that the major difficulty he had on the team was the fact that he and Lawrence had such fundamentally different starting points. While Ted trusted people until he had reason not to, Lawrence worked on the opposite basis. The result: a choice. Can two such people decide to put these differences aside and work together? I'm not sure.

But what I am sure about is that trusting in another's good intent is a solid basis for any working relationship and future success.

I hear over and over about the breakthroughs that occur as a result of team members being trusted to take accountability and make stuff happen. Recently, a CEO brought together his senior leaders to focus on shaping the company's future success. It was a meeting with a loose agenda. Consequently, people were nervous about what would happen. They were used to being told what to do, rather than being included in the thought process.

At first, team members were reluctant to step forward and share their ideas, however their leader responded to every remark with the genuine desire to learn and understand. By the end of Day 1, people were speaking up freely. The turning point came the following day when the leader focused on addressing all the points that had been made over dinner the night before. People felt genuinely heard, and their opinions taken seriously, both evidence of trust – as a consequence they showed new levels of passion and accountability in driving forward the success of the organisation.

Giving trust gains trust. It sends the powerful message to others of: *I believe in you. You have the capability to succeed. Our relationship is based on a trusted partnership.*

I recognise that things happen which can lower trust. But I do believe that most people come to work wanting to make a significant contribution and if they don't there is usually a valid reason as to why not.

Your willingness to keep extending trust is a genuine act of leadership.

Take a Lead

On a scale of 1-10, how high do you rank your 'trustability'? If it is anything less than an 8, conduct a trust audit to understand what it would take to increase the level of trust in your relationships:

- Resolve any personal issues of mistrust

- Seek feedback as to how trustworthy you are

- Be fact-based in your decision making

- Make transparency your signature

- Give trust to gain it

How do others see you?

Describe a powerful leader in one word: 'presence'.

Chapter 46

The Power of Presence

Back in 1996, when my wife and I first met, we took a trip to India in search of 'enlightenment'. Our itinerary? To visit several gurus whom we hoped would answer just a few of life's big questions:

Who am I?

What do I really want?

What is the purpose of life?

Our first stop was Dharamsala, home of the Dalai Lama. We got up at the crack of dawn in Delhi to get on the rickety bus that would take us there. Well, sitting next to a young Canadian monk who was in his way to study Buddhism over the next few months certainly helped – his calm outlook was a great distraction to the death-defying journey.

It was a very wet August, and the end of the monsoon season. Arriving in Dharamsala we were greeted with low-lying mist which dampened our spirits, rather like the only hotel room we could find. Rising at the crack of dawn, we wrapped up in our warmest things, and made the long trek in the dark up the winding paths towards the Tsuglagkhang Buddhist Temple. When, out of the mist, the Dalai Lama appeared and walked towards the crowds, our eyes connected for an instant. It was the greatest presence I have ever felt; there was a sense of recognition that went beyond time and space. It was as if he saw into the deepest core of my being. And he did that with everyone he looked at. Only someone with a truly to great sense of who they are can have such presence himself. And really 'see' those around him.

So, what is real presence?

It is the ability to suspend the constant judgment and chatter that takes place in our minds, allowing us to elevate our awareness to something greater than our individual agendas.

It is an energy that vibrates at a higher frequency causing us to have expanded sensory acuity to what is happening in the present moment.

Presence has its own intelligence. When we are 'tuned in to it' we are able to see more clearly, empathise more deeply and have a better understanding of what is happening around us.

The development of presence takes deliberate attention. Increasing your self-awareness through disciplines like meditation, prayer and reflective writing helps you to become mindful of presence.

'Being' on purpose, following your vision, and living your values provides a powerful foundation for your true presence to emerge. Building confidence and capability in your work gives you greater capacity for presence. Having the courage to be more open and honest in your relationships strengthens your presence. However, the most important way of developing a strong presence is through conscious intention. Your willingness to set a deliberate intent for presence to guide and inspire you *every day* will accelerate the growth and increase the power of your individual presence.

Oliver, the CEO of a FTSE 100 company was a man I had the privilege of watching in several settings, and a brilliant example of a leader with great presence. A true visionary, during every large conference he led, he came across with clarity, confidence and humility, showing a tremendous ability to engage and inspire others in taking the journey together. He didn't just 'talk big' either. In small meetings he listened intently and was always highly focused on creating environments in which people could make their best contribution. Whenever he walked into a room you felt his arrival simply through the quality of his presence. This quality was not an accident. Oliver had deliberately nurtured this skill, focusing his attention on developing his presence to the maximum. He had realised in his role as CEO that his ability to control situations through managing them tightly was not going to work, given the breadth of his responsibility. The most important contribution he could make would be to influence others to move in the right direction, and this influence was best developed through a strong presence, enabling his people to naturally resonate with his wavelength, rather than through the force of effort.

How would you describe your own presence? Is it a quality that you have focused on developing in the past? If so, what enabled you to do it and can you continue developing it? If not, what do you believe needs to happen in order for you to develop greater presence?

In my executive coaching programmes I encourage leaders to take the following 3 steps to increase the strength of their presence:

1. Develop a vision for your own presence

What does great presence look, sound and feel like for you? Invest the time and energy to create a compelling picture of your desired state of presence. For instance, one leader I coached created a truly aspirational vision, boiling it down as:

- My relationships are increasingly based on shared trust and respect, which raises my presence.
- My communication resonates with a sense of inner truth which means I come across with presence.
- My decision-making is guided by a sense of presence, which ensures that I do the right thing.
- I am known for having a quiet, reassuring presence that ensures others feel good about who they are and what they do.

This vision will create the clarity and energy to keep you focused on developing presence when the challenges of the day-to-day world tempt you off track.

2. Write down a Personal Development Plan (PDP) focusing on how to strengthen your presence

Zac was so obsessed with moving up the ladder of success within his organisation, that I had been called in to coach him, focusing on his progression, as his line manager clearly explained that his obsession with his advancement would be the biggest derailing force and potential barrier to it happening.

Through our conversations, Zac became increasingly clear about the implications of continuing in his egocentric approach to his career and began to be keen to embrace a different way; however he did not know what this meant in practice. I gave him the exercise to create a vision of his desired future presence in order to strengthen his current position, asking him to explain how he thought he would need to grow in order to achieve it.

We conducted a time-line map where he projected 3 years into the future and visualised where he wanted to be. Then, I asked him to look back and describe how he had changed in order to get there. He identified three key 'qualities' he needed to acquire fundamental to his growth: 1) Humility 2) Inspiration 3) Listening.

Together we broke these themes down into specific goals with action plans attached, which would enable us to track his progress. So far he is doing well, and his line manager and CEO are heartened by his progress.

Once you have identified your vision, you can get straight onto the creation of your personal development plan to support you in taking the necessary steps to bringing it to fruition.

3. Surround yourself with honest critics

A leader with strong presence has the inner security and genuine humility to request straightforward feedback and constant challenge to keep them on track. These qualities will ensure that your view of your own presence is accurately validated on a regular basis through one-to-one conversations and a personalised 360-feedback process.

Having a strong presence will energise you, enable growth and inspire others to be the best they can be.

Take a Lead

Commit to taking the 3 steps to developing your presence:

1. Create a vision that inspires you to develop strong presence.

2. Make a personal development plan focused on how to strengthen your presence.

3. Surround yourself with honest critics who will value and evaluate the quality of your presence.

What is your vision?

The greatest leaders are those with a clear vision at their core.

Chapter 47

Inspiring Vision

I'm not asking you to be a Mahatma Gandhi, Martin Luther King, Mother Teresa or even a Steve Jobs, Richard Branson or Anita Roddick. Nor any other famous visionary who has contributed to the world as we know it today.

But what I *am* asking is that you create a compelling vision that will inspire who you are and what you do; which in turn inspires others.

When I look back at my youth spent at the Yehudi Menuhin School, the biggest gift I'd say I was privileged to receive was the opportunity to be surrounded by a host of amazing guests who were invited to speak to us, and how each covered such various disciplines.

Each one of them had their own unique vision. And it rubbed off on us.

Lord Menuhin set up events, schools, festivals, charities; he was dedicated to bridging the political differences between China and the United Kingdom for example, via his vision for music as a medium for cutting through barriers. At the school we met Sally Trench, author of *Bury Me In My Boots*, whose vision for helping homeless people led her to set up Project Spark, a remarkable programme for giving troubled youths a chance in life. We were taught chamber music by Hans Keller, a survivor of the Holocaust, imbibing his philosophy, which was to create music of the highest standard.

Later on, when I found myself entering the world of personal development – my own chosen field – I was inspired by Sondra Ray, whose vision was to create a global community centred around love. Her Loving Relationships Training (LRT) taught people the essential characteristics required for building healthy and harmonious relationships. Bob Mandel, the global director of LRT travelled the planet, bringing people together to focus on resolving conflict and restoring harmony in the name of peace. My business partner for many years, Dr Robert Holden, had a personal vision to educate people about the meaning of true happiness. 'The Happiness Project' took a stand for happiness in the world, and running it together for fifteen years showed us what a difference such a concept can make in people's lives.

I have been blessed to have many entrepreneurs as friends whose personal vision has led them to make meaningful contributions in the world. Andy Thrasyvolou, founder of myhotel has a vision of where Eastern philosophy meets Western technology in his stunning boutique hotels. Simon Woodroffe, founder of Yo! Sushi never ceases to amaze me with his innovative ideas and ability to make stuff happen from sushi on conveyor belts to pods in hotels. Renée Elliott had the vision for an organic life, and her creation of Planet Organic, the largest organic supermarket in the UK, is a testimony to her deep commitment to supporting a harmonious way of eating and living.

However, being visionary does not need to translate into big achievements, high profile exploits or profitable endeavors. Take my daughter, for example, who now at 12 has a vision of beauty which expresses itself through art: whether she spends all day on a beach making stunning pictures using petals, shells, and washed up fish eggs, or creating incredible stills in her art class, India's vision is hard at play. She catches a lot of it from her mother Veronica, whose creative design sense is an innate part of her.

It's interesting to note that 'being visionary' at the organisational level is harder to find. I see that there is still a prevalent idea around that vision belongs to a lone figure at the top of a company, or perhaps stretches to the Executive Committee.

The irony here is that one of the primary attributes that top executives look for in their people is… vision.

They want to be surrounded by others who are prepared to see things differently, challenge the status quo and can paint a picture of the organisation's future – in short, who are innovative. So if vision is so vital why is it so scarce?

I believe it is because our modern Western society has created a sausage factory, which chips away at people's inherent ability to embrace their own vision. For instance, although my children attend good schools, the educational system here in the UK dictates that schools put the emphasis on IQ over and above the development of less tangible skills such as spiritual intelligence, which is directly related to vision. Observing my children's education is a classic case of watching their personal vision getting knocked out of them at an early age. I personally struggle with the dilemma of having them in a system that measures their academic results over and above their emotional, social and spiritual intelligence. In order to compensate, I do whatever I can to develop their 'other sides' outside of school – their creativity of thought, innate vision of life and originality.

Going through the education system, the majority of us sit down with career advisors who give us well-intentioned options.

But they are not visionary.

Rather than being encouraged to discover our true purpose and see how it can inspire our service to the world, we get boxed into thinking a career is about a particular skill set, sector or financial target. It is no wonder that I witness a form of corporate slavery, where people get locked into roles through financial ties, or the promise of future promotion. If you are in a similar position, you need to ask yourself, *If it weren't about the money, would I devote 60-80 hours a week doing what I do?*

It's not that money is wrong. It's simply not enough of a vision, not enough to inspire.

Another significant factor that diminishes our personal vision is our consumer economy, which persuades us what to believe in order to be happy, successful, healthy and fulfilled. We are bombarded with millions of messages telling us what we think we want. Coke sells enjoyment. Pure pleasure is to be found in a BMW. If it's love you're looking for, then head off to McDonalds, and visit Disney if you want happiness. All these brands are vying to gain valuable market share in your sphere of vision.

Make *your* vision a priority.

Dedicate precious time to nurturing and discovering what it is. Find your own way to making that vision the central part of your leadership. Have you heard of a vision quest? You simply take yourself out of your normal habitat and into one that has different stimuli in order to challenge your latent visionary ability. One leader I know took his team to India and Africa where they supported local communities in building homes, schools and water wells. They used these powerful experiences to test their own paradigms of work and life, allowing a more creative approach in challenging situations. Another leader put on monthly lunches for his company, inviting a wide range of speakers to talk about thought-provoking, and not just business-related, topics. Other great leaders find their vision through more reflective practices – reading, writing and meditation.

Select a moment in time, say 1-3 years from now and ask yourself, *What do I want to see, feel and hear that will truly inspire me?* Write your vision in the present tense as if it is already happening by using *I am* statements as opposed to future statements such as *I will* or *I want*. These statements of intent begin to shape your reality. Use the four Intelligences: Physical, Emotional, Intellectual and Spiritual as a mirror to look through. For instance, a 3-year vision could include the following themes:

PHYSICAL	EMOTIONAL
• I am energised and energise others. • I enjoy vibrant health and well-being. • I have high personal impact that lights up a room when I walk into it.	• I have true personal and social awareness, which ensures that I am attuned to all situations. • I enjoy deep and meaningful relationships in all areas of my life. • I am highly influential through my authentic presence.

INTELLECTUAL	SPIRITUAL
• I am clear about the direction in which I'm headed, and I make the right decisions. • I stretch myself creatively to generate innovative solutions. • I have time and space to think.	• I am purpose-led in my life, work and relationships. • I derive great meaning from who I am, what I do and what I accomplish. • I am inspired and inspire others.

As you create the vision you want, it becomes more compelling.

The ultimate test of your vision is how much it inspires you. Simply put, if your vision doesn't make you want to jump out of bed in the morning, get another one.

Take a Lead

Set aside time to develop your vision.

- Start with creating a compelling one-year vision.

- Make sure you read your vision at least once a month to energise and stay connected to it.

- Share it with a close confidante who can support and challenge you to follow it.

Change is Inevitable

'Be the change that you want to see in the world' – Gandhi

Chapter 48

Change Happens

I once worked in a company that was facing a major crisis.

It was an iconic brand in the UK economy and had an air of invincibility about it. That is, until major changes were forced on the industry in general – and the company had to either change, or fold.

The Executive Committee came together, determined to provide the right leadership during this time of unprecedented change. The plan was to change the business model from being product-focused to a more customer-focused one: the people had to change, moving from a top-heavy structure to a lighter senior leadership population; and the operating model had to change, moving from a rigid format to a more agile way of working. There were only a few of the Executive that had led such an unprecedented move before, and as a consequence faced high levels of anxiety as to how things should move ahead.

Together with the HR Director, I put together an initial plan to help the Executive Committee gain clarity and alignment as to *how* to lead the change within the organisation. We started off with a check-list of six key factors to be put into place.

1. To create a compelling case for change – provide a clear and simple narrative.
2. To provide visible and transparent leadership – be open and honest, available to listen and understand.
3. To ensure that everyone has the right information and resources in order to make the right decisions – communicate frequently and offer support.
4. To empower action – build capability and confidence around the required change.
5. To deliver short term wins – recognise success and manage underperformance swiftly.
6. To follow through – make the change stick.

We also prepared the Executive for the emotional cycle of change so that they could reflect on what their people would be going through:

- *Shock* – disbelief that change is happening which can cause behaviours of denial, avoidance and emotional shut down.
- *Resistance* – active push-back against the change, failure to embrace it, or demonstration of passive aggressive behaviour.
- *Disengagement* – people 'checking out' physically, emotionally, intellectually or spiritually as a form of protection and self-preservation.
- *Exploration* – if people have been supported in the right way they will start to inquire about the opportunity change provides, resilience will kick in and a learning mindset develops.
- *Commitment* – change is accepted, engagement has returned and people are determined to make the change happen and build upon the learning.

Most interesting to see was the positive effect on the

Executive who, in an open environment, had the opportunity to share where they were on a personal level, and to work out how they could support each other, as well as their people. This gave them the solid foundation they needed in order to front the organisation with the clarity and confidence that is so essential during changing times.

Change is inevitable.

It doesn't matter the strength of your brand, the brilliance of your people or the effectiveness of your delivery, change happens. I have found that some leaders thrive on change. They abhor the status quo and constantly strive to make changes for the better. Other leaders are more resistant to change. They try and hold on to the past as a reference point for the future. Wherever you stand, your ability to lead change effectively is one of the most important areas you can develop as a leader.

Let's look at the six points in more depth:

1. Create a compelling case for change – provide a clear and simple narrative.

This is a critical starting point. Unless people understand the purpose of change, the *why* of it, then resistance will very quickly kick in. Nobody likes change for change's sake. It's a waste of precious time, energy and resources. It's essential that change is either a result of an inspiring vision, or a burning platform. Many of the greatest organisational success stories today such as Apple, Amazon, Starbucks, P&G and Unilever were created by inspiring visions that drove the required changes, turning them into industry-leading companies. On the other hand, one can see that burning platforms for change transformed businesses like IBM, McDonald's, Samsung and BP.

The success criteria for the narrative should address the 4 Intelligences:

A. Energy. *Will the narrative energise people?* (Physical Intelligence)

B. Engagement. *Will the narrative emotionally engage people?* (Emotional Intelligence)

C. Clarity. *Does the narrative provide a clear direction?* (Intellectual Intelligence)

D. Inspiration. *Does the narrative inspire people to grow?* (Spiritual Intelligence)

2. Provide visible and transparent leadership – be open and honest, listen and understand.

One of the biggest mistakes a leader can make during times of change is to hide. Unfortunately, I have witnessed too many so-called leaders 'going undercover' and failing to provide the hands-on leadership required when uncertainty hits. The best leaders increase their level of visibility and transparency in an organisation during times of change so that people can feel seen, heard and understood.

Debra had been on the wrong side of several failed change programmes in the past, so when she was finally in a position to lead an organisational department she was determined to do it differently. Once the narrative about the change agenda had been created and signed-off with her Executive colleagues, she immediately called a meeting with her leadership team in order to take them through the business case for the changes ahead. Then she created the space for everyone around the table to share their point of view, how they were feeling and to answer any questions they had.

Having brought the team together, Debra then set up a series of personal meetings with each team member to debrief them further about their own position and confirm what they needed from her. The next step was to quickly organise a Town Hall for all employees to ensure that no rumours got out and that everyone heard the same message at the same time. There Debra spoke candidly and from the heart, sharing the facts and how she felt about the impending changes. The leadership team gave their perspective and there was an open Q&A session in order to create an inclusive and collaborative environment.

Over the next 90 days, Debora kept up a relentless schedule of walking the floors, and ensuring people had access to her diary in order to create an open dialogue. This approach went a long way to ensuring the most successful period of change in the history of the organisation.

3. Ensure people have the right information and resources to be able to make the right decisions – communicate frequently and offer support.

A few years ago, in mid-December, I got a last-minute request to support a team who were on the verge of leading a major change initiative. I sent out a few quick e-mails to get a temperature gauge of the various team members. The response caused me real concern. They had different information about the scale and timing of the change, and there was low trust about the leader's ability to lead the change programme effectively. Most significantly, there were rumours that redundancies would impact the team, but no one knew what the basis of the decision-making process would be.

Their leader, David, was an intimidating character with the tendency to dominate using a very controlling style, so I faced an extremely uncomfortable moment in giving him the feedback from my early findings. I remember telling myself that if I was fired in the heat of the moment, at least he'd know what was going on for his people. But luckily he was able to put his ego aside and surprised me by listening to the comments. He pushed back hard, but I insisted that he should follow up and check the facts. He agreed to sit down with his HR Business Partner, who confirmed my findings and recommended that he go back to the team and follow the process by the book to ensure that everyone would have the right information and resources to be able to get through Christmas. Once they reconvened early in the New Year, I followed up with the team to understand the progress made and although they were at the beginning of the change journey, at least they were on the same page with information and support.

One of the biggest traps that leaders fall into is assuming people are up to speed with exactly what's going on: both the level of information and the thought processes involved. It's vital to remember that just because you have the facts and have been very close to the planning process it doesn't mean that others are, and they simply can't be in the picture until you let them see it.

4. Empower action – build capability and confidence around the required change.

The nature of change is that it triggers anxiety, which once kicked in tends to delay action. This is the exact opposite of what is required in times of change, when it is essential to act swiftly and decisively. Andy is a master of change. As soon as he gets wind of needing to make a change he takes action to make it happen. On one occasion he had recruited a great MD to run his business. The MD was doing a good job but was on the verge of leaving due to his frustration with the organisational structure. Andy called his senior team together, explained the situation, set out his expectations and then empowered the team to come up with the right solutions and act on them. This approach unleashed a wave of energy in the team who went back to the drawing board to create a new organisational design which met the exact needs of the new MD. Although no one on the team was a recognised organisational expert, the empowerment Andy gave them ensured that new capability and confidence could be engineered.

I am a firm believer that if you treat people as capable, resourceful and thoughtful you will get constructive behaviour in return. Empower people and they will act empowered. Compromise people's ability to act and you will get diminished returns.

5. Deliver short term wins – recognise success and manage underperformance swiftly.

There is no better antidote to the possible disengagement that can accompany change than achieving some quick wins. I was coaching a bold leader, who mid-way through a financial year realised that he was not winning. It was a big wake-up call and resulted in Phillip having to make some fundamental changes in the way the business operated. He realised that these changes amounted to a cultural change, and would not happen overnight. In fact, they'd probably be met by great resistance in the business. He recognised that he had to deliver some short term wins in order to build buy-in and belief for the journey ahead.

Phillip called his leadership team together to examine what they could do to make a measurable shift in the business. They saw that the greatest difference they could immediately make would be to focus on customer satisfaction. Collectively they reprioritised their time and attention, focusing the majority of it on implementing some creative ways of boosting the quality and care that their customers received. The initiative delivered. Almost overnight their customer satisfaction scores began rising. This captured the imagination of employees, who got caught on the wave of excitement it generated. The leader followed up by celebrating the initial success. He also tightened the way performance was managed in the organisation by implementing consequences for those who did not step up and make the necessary changes, in order for performance to turn around. Within twelve months, Phillip's efforts had doubled business performance, giving him the opportunity to focus on creating longer term sustainable change.

6. Follow through – make the change stick.

The first time I met Bruce, he made it clear that one of his biggest passions was the importance of follow up, and his subsequent high frustration levels when it was lacking. He believed that the reason most change efforts failed was due to the lack of follow-up. It was the reason he called me in – to address the frustration he felt regarding his team not taking sufficient accountability for making change stick. Bruce wanted to understand why this occurred and what he needed to do differently in order to create an environment in which people would be committed to relentless follow-through.

My diagnostic interviews with his team focused heavily on this dilemma. What transpired was that although people were committed to making change, they saw others as being ultimately responsible and accountable for it, and usually those more senior. Given this view, they would take their eye of the ball at the crucial moment, and just when everyone needed to get over the line. Although Bruce had discussed the issue with them it was usually in the heat of the moment of his frustration, which inhibited their ability to create practical solutions to work with.

When I debriefed Bruce on these findings, the situation suddenly became as clear as day to him. He saw how his frustration took over and clouded the vital message – which was that everyone had to be accountable for follow up. He was then able to go back to his team, share the findings and take everyone on a journey of mutual accountability for making change stick.

At the end of the day change is a messy business. You can have the best-laid plans in the world, but you cannot always predict the outcome. Sometimes those who you believe will respond well to change wobble, whilst the least expected rise to the challenge.

The key to successful change is to lead by example so that others will be inspired to rise to its challenge.

Take a Lead

Assess yourself against the six factors for leading change. On a scale of 1-5, (1=very low; 5=very high) how effective are you at:

1. Creating a compelling case for change – having a clear and simple narrative.

2. Providing visible and transparent leadership – being open and honest, listening to understand.

3. Ensuring that everyone has the right information and resources in order to make the right decisions – communicating frequently and offering support.

4. Empowering action – building capability and confidence around the required change.

5. Delivering short term wins – recognising success and managing underperformance swiftly.

6. Following through – making the change stick.

Ask yourself: *What do I need to do more, less or differently to become an expert at leading change?*

Do you prioritise your priorities? Really?

The point of leadership is to make sure that what's important stays important.

Chapter 49

Prioritise!

I started *LEAD!* showing a picture of our sped-up lives in a world filled with distraction, interruption and interference – taking us away from leading an inspired life and from being the best we can be.

Now, as we come to the end of the book, I know that all those factors are still very present. Our inboxes are filled daily. Back-to-back meetings are scheduled well in advance. The relentless pressure to deliver tangible results gets higher day by day.

The need to define what matters most, and keep it at the top of your priority list, is the real task at hand.

So, how do we work out what that is?

Hopefully, each chapter so far has encouraged you to clarify in more depth what matters most to you. However, to simplify it, below is a breakdown of the four fundamental priorities, which have been a running thread throughout the book:

1. Physical priorities

Writing this book, what mattered most to me was ensuring I had the enduring energy to start and complete it. In previous years

I had put my writing on hold due to the enormous demands of a self-sustained career which included flying around the globe coaching top leaders, nurturing a home life with a loving partner and being father to three growing children.

In a nutshell, I was knackered!

At the end of the day, I had very little energy to sit down and write. So I began jogging to recharge my batteries. However, I started picking up small injuries, and given that my recovery rate was not what it used to be, I headed back to the gym. Not my first choice, as I'd rather be outside than surrounded by TV screens. But what mattered most was to sustain my energy, and I knew that regular exercise would make a big difference. I decided to exercise daily so as to avoid the temptation to procrastinate, and found that the cross-trainer was the best machine for me, giving me aerobic exercise and enabling me to read inspiring literature at the same time.

Practicing pilates, even for just ten minutes a day, has allowed me to get in touch with a deeper energy through the breath, and by doing so, strengthens my core.

So, what are your physical priorities? Is it more energy? Increased vitality? Better well-being?

It is your responsibility to nourish and refine those physical priorities – and that includes your nutrition, sleep, hydration and relaxation. I know this appears basic and it is; however by not prioritising these vital physical needs, you will run into trouble.

2. Emotional priorities

The deepest needs we have as human beings are to be recognised, valued and loved. There is no doubt that when we are genuinely appreciated for who we are, we feel whole and happy.

So, what is the key to getting your emotional needs met? I believe it is by taking responsibility for them so that you don't become emotionally needy. Which, as we know is a real turn-off – both in our personal as well as professional relationships. I have witnessed countless occasions where a team member will look to their leader for validation in such a way as to cause it to backfire and the leader to move away. This is in contrast to a team player who is self-reliant and able to accurately assess their own value, approaching the leader in a self-contained way. The leader is then far more likely to reach out and provide the recognition or understanding that is needed.

I find the most helpful tool in managing emotional needs is by keeping a journal – writing down your fears, dreams, hopes, frustrations, challenges and observations. A journal will provide you with a constructive space to 'download' your thinking, deepen your reflections and disclose your issues in such a way that puts no baggage on anyone else. My journal of choice is the legendary black moleskin notebook that artists and thinkers have used down the centuries, from Vincent van Gogh and Pablo Picasso to Ernest Hemingway and Bruce Chatwin – my own one inspires me to write virtually every day.

3. Intellectual priorities

As a leader what matters most is the *quality* of your thinking. There is a direct correlation between the quality of your thinking and the quality of your actions. Smart thinking leads to smart results.

However, I notice that most leaders fail to prioritise 'think time' and simply keep busy. It is fundamental to ask yourself: *When and where I do my best thinking?*

The response I usually hear is: while jogging, in the shower, gardening, walking the dog, reading and travelling. I have never come across anyone who has claimed that they do their best thinking in the office! Make sure that quality think-time becomes a non-negotiable part of your life. Nourishing your thinking leads to more creativity, greater clarity, better decision making, enriching conversations and smarter actions. Schedule at least 5 minutes a day for thinking. This could take the form of keeping a journal, having some time off, reading inspirational literature, or a quiet walk. I will guarantee that if you make the commitment to think better thoughts than you did yesterday you will meet your mind's true needs.

4. Spiritual priorities

Chip Conley, founder and former CEO of Joie de Vivre boutique hotel company, is an inspiring example of someone who focused on making his spiritual needs a priority – and as a consequence transformed a company. After fifteen years of rising to the pinnacle of the hospitality industry, Joie de Vivre was suddenly undercapitalised and over-exposed in the post dot.com, post 9/11 economy. For relief and inspiration, Conley, turned to psychologist Abraham Maslow's iconic 'hierarchy of needs' and overcame the storm that had hit the travel industry.

In Conley's impressive book *PEAK: How Great Companies get their Mojo from Maslow*, he describes how he climbed Maslow's different levels of need, and was able to create a remarkable turnaround in himself and his company. At the top of Maslow's hierarchy is self-actualisation, which he describes as *'What a man can be, he must be.'* For me, this captures the importance of prioritising your spiritual needs in a nutshell.

Make your spiritual needs a priority by incorporating the following factors:

- Discovering and living your purpose
- Understanding and honouring your values
- Having a clear sense of meaning in your work and life
- Being authentic
- Applying compassion and forgiveness in relationships
- Committing to living an inspired life

Your ability to prioritise and meet your spiritual needs will move you from a place of transaction to a state of transformation. In order to do so, it demands that you answer questions like: *Why do I do what I do? What is my purpose? What are my core values? What is the difference I want to make? How do I want to serve? What inspires me?*

Make sure you keep revisiting these questions until you have the necessary clarity to know what matters most. To *you*. Summing it up: Leadership is the ability to stay focused on your priorities.

Take a Lead

Every day ask yourself, *What matters most today?*
It is a powerful reminder to focus on what's most
important.

- My physical priorities

- My emotional priorities

- My intellectual priorities

- My spiritual priorities

The idea of servant as leader

'Do they, while being served, become healthier, wiser, freer, more autonomous, more likely themselves to become servants?'

Chapter 50

To Serve is To Lead

I sat in my office on a cold, gray and wet January day. Having just returned from a month visiting my wife's family in the beauty of New Zealand, I simply could not face the prospect of powering up my laptop and going through what awaited me there.

I had finished the year before burnt out, and had no desire to return to what I had been doing. In that moment I made a life-altering decision. I quit. I literally handed my notice in to myself. It was a little awkward as I wasn't sure about any kind of closing ceremony, but I knew that I would never go back to work again in the way that I had known it.

The following morning, I sat down with a pad and paper and wrote down what was truly meaningful for me. I knew that what I love to do is to serve. And for me, service is about making a difference in people's lives. I broke that down as:

- Understanding and meeting the needs of others in order to improve their lives
- Creating the right environment in which others can learn and grow

- Enabling people to be the best version of themselves
- Inspiring others to remember what's most important

From that day on, I no longer worked in the traditional sense; I didn't have a regular job, I stopped working all hours and I never felt obligated or compromised into doing anything I didn't want to do. Committing myself to 'serve' opened up a whole new world of possibilities.

Service is a misunderstood concept.

It has connotations of sacrifice, subservience and low paid work. Yet nothing could be further from the truth. Real service is one of the highest forms of expressing one's purpose and passion. It is the tangible evidence of a humility and willingness to help others. Through selfless service, displayed with a profound commitment to the common good and to the sustainability of future generations, everyone benefits. Service directly challenges our dog-eat-dog, competitive world where so many people are out for their own personal gain, often at the expense of others.

Let's understand the power of putting the philosophy of service and leadership together.

This is what Robert Greenleaf did, the founder of the modern 'Servant Leadership' movement in 1970. After 40 years of research on leadership, development and education whilst working for AT&T in America, Robert went on to create the Greenleaf Center for Servant Leadership. According to his essay, 'Essentials of Servant Leadership', Greenleaf's philosophy had its roots in a piece of fiction.

He writes:

> 'The idea of the servant as leader came out of reading Hermann Hesse's Journey to the East. In this story, we see a band of men on a mythical journey. The central figure of the story is Leo, who accompanies the party

as the servant who does their menial chores, but who
also sustains them with his spirit and his song. He is a
person of extraordinary presence. All goes well until Leo
disappears. Then the group falls into disarray and the
journey is abandoned. They cannot make it without the
servant Leo. The narrator, one of the party, after some
years of wandering, finds Leo and is taken into the Order
that had sponsored the journey. There he discovers that
Leo, whom he had known first as servant, was in fact the
titular head of the Order, its guiding spirit, a great and
noble leader.'

At the heart of Greenleaf's remarkable philosophy on
Servant-Leadership is the following:

'The servant-leader is servant first. Becoming a
servant-leader begins with the natural feeling that one
wants to serve, to serve first. Then conscious choice
brings one to aspire to lead. That person is sharply
different from one who is leader first. The difference
manifests itself in the care taken by the servant first to
make sure that other people's highest priority needs
are being served. The best test, and the most difficult to
administer, is this: Do those served grow as persons? Do
they, while being served, become healthier, wiser, freer,
more autonomous, more likely themselves to become
servants?'

I had the privilege of coaching Jeremy, a leader who
embodies the servant-leader principle. A true humanitarian,
Jeremy is committed to serving his organisation, his people,
his customers and his shareholders. His generous spirit,
thoughtful actions and compassionate decision-making
make him one of a kind. When there are performance issues

in the company, he will give people the benefit of the doubt, taking into consideration the full contribution that they have made over the years and focusing on removing any interference that stops them performing at their best, rather than having a knee-jerk reaction such has firing them or micro-managing. As a result, people love working for him. It generates tremendous loyalty, creates an environment of sustainable success and delivers outstanding business results.

I'm often challenged about the subject of servant-leadership as a weak position, which compromises our ability to make tough decisions. I witness the opposite. Someone who is committed to serving makes the hard calls that leaders need to make, the difference often being that they do it in such a way which takes people with them. For instance, when the financial crisis hit in 2008, Jeremy had to reduce his head count by over 20%. This was the most traumatic challenge of his leadership tenure, but because people had such great respect for him as a leader, they understood the position he faced and trusted his judgment. Staying true to his service principles, he was able to conduct a transparent redundancy programme, allowing those who left the firm to do so with a sense of appreciation and understanding, many of whom still reach out to him for advice, based on the fact that he strove so hard to do the right thing.

A life of service provides a context and meaning to all things – including our work, family, relationships and community, which transcends day-to-day task. By becoming servant-leaders we lift ourselves up, focus on the bigger picture and give our best. Again and again.

A life of service is a life worth living.

Take a Lead

Reflect upon what service means to you.

Consider the idea of shifting your paradigm of work to one of service. Your paradigm of getting to giving. Your paradigm of competing to cooperating.

Each day ask yourself:

- How can I serve today?
- What would I be doing differently if I were genuinely servicing my customers?
- My team?
- My boss?
- My colleagues?
- My community?
- My family?
- My friends?
- Myself?

Create your future today

Leadership happens by focusing on what's most important.

All the time.

Conclusion

Every major turning point, event and experience in my life has had one thing in common – it has been an act of leadership:

- Leaving the music world to follow my passion for psychology and personal development
- Asking my wife, Veronica, to marry me
- Travelling to India in search of enlightenment
- Learning to meditate
- Having three amazing children
- Purchasing our dream London home
- Becoming an author
- Designing leadership development programmes for FTSE 100 companies
- Coaching top leaders around the globe

I am sure your life has followed a similar pattern.

Think about it.

Each game-changing decision you have made has been the result of taking the lead in your own life, work and relationships by focusing on what's most important *at that moment in time*. This is the way we create our future.

We create it by:

- Knowing what is most important
- Focusing wholeheartedly on it
- Allowing no distractions
- Influencing others to support us
- Tracking our progress and adjusting our course where necessary
- Continuing to learn and discover
- Celebrating along the way

The challenge is to know what's most important. Reading *LEAD!* has hopefully enhanced your clarity about what you want to change. By focusing on the following 4 key elements it will ensure that you will create sustainable change for a better future.

1. **INTENTION** inspires outcome. As outlined in Chapter 5, we saw that in order to lead well, you must clarify your primary intention. Whether it is:

- To inspire
- To connect
- To grow
- To serve
- To love

Ask yourself, *What is my intention?*

2. **VISION**. In Chapter 47, I highlighted the importance of having a compelling leadership vision. Bottom line – if your current vision doesn't inspire, then create another one! As you develop your vision, it will require you to suspend judgment as to how you will achieve it. Put your

energy, attention and focus on what you want to create; your vision has its own innate intelligence which will pull you in the right direction. If you are clear enough about what it is that you want to manifest – and have unwavering faith that you will get there – the universe will conspire to support you. *What is your vision?*

3. **SKILL SET**. The range of skills that will bring your leadership to life includes: self-knowledge, self-management, social awareness and social abilities. Honing your skills means a lifelong commitment to continuing learning and self-improvement. Take the example of Colin Matthews, former CEO of Heathrow, dedicated to the philosophy of continuous improvement. When he took over the running of Heathrow, the company had just come out of the difficulties of opening Terminal 5. Confidence was shattered. Processes had broken down. The airport had lost its identity. As I write this, six years later, Heathrow has just opened Terminal 2, the Queen's Terminal, and Terminal 5 has won best airport terminal by Skytrax World Airport Awards. I have been fortunate enough to watch Colin's relentless pursuit of continuous improvement now embedded in the company purpose, *Making Every Journey Better*. Watch out for the tendency to overestimate what you can achieve in a year, and to underestimate what you can achieve in a decade. Commit to becoming better every day. *What skills do you need to improve?*

4. **ACTION.** As Nelson Mandela so memorably said: *'Action without vision is only passing time, vision without action is merely daydreaming, but vision with action can change the world.'* This sums up where you go from here. Act on what's most important. Act on what is in your heart. Act on creating your vision. Act on improving your skills. One

of the most distinguishing marks of a great leader is the ability to make thing happen. Get things done. Execute effectively. Inspire others to act. Ask yourself, *What action do I need to take?*

At the end of the day it is your willingness to lead that inspires you and others.

Don't wait until you believe the conditions of your life are right to take a lead.

Don't put off what you could be living today.

Don't expect everything to fall into place immediately.

As you tap into your leadership potential, you will reap the rewards of being stretched, of growing and of becoming the best version of yourself.

Take the lead in your own life.

Ben Renshaw

Inspiration

Below is an essential list of resources to inspire your learning and development going forward:

Leadership Practices

1. **Reflection.** Schedule think time to increase the quality of your, clarity, direction and decision-making.
2. **Journaling.** Make a note of your learning, observations, challenges and ideas.
3. **Storytelling.** Share stories to build an emotional connection with others.
4. **Conversation.** Engage in meaningful conversation to build alignment, create opportunities, drive action and deliver results.
5. **Coaching & Mentoring.** Bring out the best in yourself and others through personal development.
6. **Feedback.** Give and receive constructive feedback to encourage continual improvement.
7. **Listening.** Commit to empathetic listening in order to understand others.
8. **Visioning.** Create a compelling picture of your desired future state.
9. **Mindfulness.** Practise sitting quietly for a minimum of 5 minutes each day and observe the breath as a focal point.
10. **Celebration.** Make a habit of recognising and celebrating success.

Leadership Books

1. *The 3rd Alternative* by Stephen R. Covey
2. *The Daily Drucker* by Peter Drucker with Joseph A. Maciariello
3. *The Art of Being* by Erich Fromm
4. *Authentic Leadership* by Bill George
5. *Servant Leadership* by Robert K. Greenleaf and Larry C. Spears
6. *Authentic Success* by Robert Holden
7. *Synchronicity* by Joseph Jaworski
8. *Strengths Based Leadership* by Tom Rath and Barry Conchie
9. *Presence* by Peter M. Senge, Joseph Jaworski, C. Otto Scharmer and Betty Sue Flowers
10. *The Leader Who Had No Title* by Robin S. Sharma

Leadership Articles, Harvard Business Review

1. 'How Will You Measure Your Life?' Clayton M. Christensen
2. 'Level 5 Leadership' Jim Collins
3. 'Managing Oneself' Peter F Drucker
4. 'Managing Authenticity' Rob Goffee and Gareth Jones
5. 'Why Should Anyone Be Led by You?' Rob Goffee and Gareth Jones
6. 'Leadership That Gets Results' Daniel Goleman
7. 'Social Intelligence and The Biology of Leadership' Daniel Goleman and Richard Boyatzis
8. 'The Making of A Corporate Athlete' Jim Loehr and Tony Schwartz
9. 'The Set Up-to-Fail Syndrome' Jean-Francois Manzoni and Jean-Louis Barsoux
10. 'Manage Your Energy, Not Your Time' Tony Schwartz and Catherine McCarthy

Online Leadership Tools

1. www.druckerinstitute.com
2. www.enneagraminstitute.com
3. www.fastcompany.com
4. www.gallup.com
5. www.hbr.org
6. www.inspiredleadership.org.uk
7. www.robertholden.org
8. www.tompeters.com
9. www.worldbusiness.org
10. www.sethgodin.com

About the Author

Ben Renshaw's innovative work – bringing out the best in people – has brought him international acclaim. He designs and delivers inspirational keynotes, bespoke senior leadership programmes, executive coaching and top team development for organisations such as Barclays, BT, Cadbury, Coca-Cola, Heathrow, Heinz, InterContinental Hotels Group, KPMG, Marks & Spencer, Nationwide, Rolls Royce, Shell, Sky, Unilever, Virgin and Zurich.

Ben is the author of seven titles, which have been translated into over 12 languages. His work has been featured in several national campaigns, covering vital concepts such as success, happiness, relationships and wellbeing – by companies from Boots and BUPA, to Kodak, P&G and Vodafone. He was the relationship expert for a Channel 4 award-winning show and has made television appearances on Newsnight, BBC News and Open University.

For further information visit: **www.benrenshaw.com**

To contact Ben: **info@benrenshaw.com**